The *Social Studies Teacher's* BOOK OF LISTS

WITH READY-TO-USE TEACHING IDEAS & ACTIVITIES

Ronald L. Partin

PRENTICE HALL
Paramus, New Jersey 07652

Library of Congress Cataloging-in-Publication Data

Partin, Ronald L.
    The social studies teacher's book of lists : with ready-to-use
teaching ideas & activities / Ronald L. Partin.
      p.   cm.
    Includes index.
    ISBN 0-13-824970-9
    1. Social sciences—Study and teaching (Elementary)—United
States—Handbook, manuals. etc.   2. Social Sciences—Study and
teaching (Secondary)—United States—Handbooks, manuals, etc.
3. Teaching—Aids and devices—Handbooks, manuals, etc.   4. Activity programs in education—United States—Handbooks, manuals, etc.   I. Title.
LB1584.P29   1992
300'.71'073—dc20

Printed in the United States of America

10   9   8

ISBN 0-13-824970-9

ATTENTION: CORPORATIONS AND SCHOOLS

Prentice Hall books are available at quantity discounts with bulk purchase for
educational, business, or sales promotional use. For information, please write to:
Prentice Hall Special Sales, 240 Frisch Court, Paramus, New Jersey 07652.
Please supply: title of book, ISBN number, quantity, how the book will be used,
date needed.

PRENTICE HALL
Paramus, NJ 07652

A Simon & Schuster Company

On the World Wide Web at http://www.phdirect.com

Prentice-Hall International (UK) Limited, *London*
Prentice-Hall of Australia Pty. Limited, *Sydney*
Prentice-Hall Canada Inc., *Toronto*
Prentice-Hall Hispanoamericana, S.A., *Mexico*
Prentice-Hall of India Private Limited, *New Delhi*
Prentice-Hall of Japan, Inc., *Tokyo*
Simon & Schuster Asia Pte. Ltd., *Singapore*
Editora Prentice-Hall do Brasil, Ltda., *Rio de Janeiro*

About This Book

Learning social studies can be fun while at the same time intellectually stimulating and practical. Yet researching and compiling the facts, activities, and ideas which bring the social studies to life takes time and effort. The lack of sufficient planning time and the scarcity of ready-to-use materials challenge all social studies teachers.

The Social Studies Teacher's Book of Lists gives you a broad range of interesting and challenging information to use in teaching United States history, world history, American government, sociology, consumer economics, psychology, and geography. It is packed with illuminating facts, startling statistics, practical checklists, and relevant research findings, which will enhance your social studies courses. The array of lists can be adapted for use with students from the 4th through 12th grades.

For easy access and use, the 379 lists in this resource are printed in a reproducible form, numbered consecutively, and organized into the following seven sections:

I.   LISTS FOR UNITED STATES HISTORY (Lists 1–104)

II.   LISTS FOR WORLD HISTORY (Lists 105–161)

III. LISTS FOR AMERICAN GOVERNMENT (Lists 162–195)

IV. LISTS FOR CONSUMER ECONOMICS (Lists 196–226)

V.   LISTS FOR SOCIOLOGY (Lists 227–281)

VI. LISTS FOR PSYCHOLOGY (Lists 282–336)

VII. LISTS FOR GEOGRAPHY (Lists 337–379)

In addition, a special introductory section presents a variety of stimulating activities for introducing the lists into your lessons to spark students' interest and enthusiasm. Each activity is accompanied by detailed directions and specific list suggestions for its effective use.

The possibilities for using the lists are limited only by the imagination. Many can be reproduced and used to encourage thoughtful discussion and problem solving (e.g., How many things can students list which were around in 1960 but are hard to find today?). Develop cooperative learning by having small groups see how many students predict the contents of a list before you present it (e.g., Which are the hottest job prospects for the coming decade?). Challenge individuals or teams to complete their own lists (e.g., How many American Indian tribes can they list? Or, what celebrities have died from drug overdoses?).

Lists can be used not only to illustrate important points in your lesson, but also to provide practice in interpreting data and as a springboard for discussion. Lists of frequently used terms (e.g., "Forms of Government" or "Therapeutic Techniques") can be used as student handouts for instant review. Some lists make stimulating posters or can be distributed as "sponge" activities for students to ponder as they wait for class to begin or when they finish an in-class assignment. Incorporate the lists into simulation and query games, such as the classroom versions of *Jeopardy* and *Family Feud* described in the introduction, "Suggestions for Using the Lists." Learning centers can also incorporate lists for interpretation and problem solving.

Most importantly, design your own creative uses of these lists to add spice and variety to your lessons. Use them to expand, enrich, enliven and excite your social studies classes.

Ronald L. Partin

About the Author

Ronald L. Partin, Ph.D., is Professor of Educational Foundations and Inquiry and Coordinator of the Guidance and Counseling Program at Bowling Green State University. As a counselor educator, he has taught courses in counseling, educational consultation, group dynamics, and learning psychology. A former high school teacher and coach, Dr. Partin has taught social studies for eight years. Dr. Partin has presented over two hundred workshops and seminars to schools throughout Ohio. In addition to numerous journal articles, Dr. Partin has coauthored *P.R.I.D.E.*, a training program on effective classroom management, which has been completed by over thirty thousand teachers nationwide. He is also coauthor of *The Social Studies Teacher's Survival Kit* (West Nyack, NY: The Center for Applied Research in Education, 1988).

To my wife, Jan

Contents

Section II LISTS FOR WORLD HISTORY

Section III LISTS FOR AMERICAN GOVERNMENT

Section IV LISTS FOR CONSUMER ECONOMICS

Section VI LISTS FOR PSYCHOLOGY

Section VII LISTS FOR GEOGRAPHY

Appendix   NEW LISTS

How to Use the Lists in This Book

The lists in this book may be used in a spectrum of creative learning activities to enrich and enliven the social studies. Generally, it is not suggested that they be memorized or used as test material. While many teachers would expect their students to know the content or some lists such as the states and capitals (No. 343) or the items of the Bill of Rights (No. 164), it is hoped that the lists will be used primarily to stimulate students' thinking, to spark enthusiasm for the social studies, to invite discussion, and to challenge students' assumptions and attitudes.

The following provides a variety of specific suggestions for using *The Social Studies Teacher's Book of Lists* with your students. With imagination you can create other uses. Your students may even suggest possible learning activities incorporating lists. Experiment, adapt, and refine. Classes differ. The same activity may not work the same with two seemingly identical classes. Also employ a variety of approaches. The element of surprise can be a most valuable motivator.

Classroom Challenge

This activity is adapted from the television game show *Family Feud*. It can be played with two or more teams of 4-6 persons each.

Preparation:

In bold letters at least 2 inches high, print each list on newsprint or cardboard. Cover each individual item with a strip of paper which is attached lightly so that the strip can be removed easily. Leave the title of the list uncovered. Make a master copy of each list so that individual items can be uncovered as they are correctly identified.

Directions:

Select 2-4 teams of 5-6 students. Try to assure that the teams are about equal in academic ability. Hang the list on the front wall so that all will be able to read it. The teams stand or are seated on either side so that they do not block the view of the list by the non-participants. The individual items of the list are each covered with their slips of paper. Appoint a scorekeeper and an assistant to reveal the individual items on the list as they are correctly identified. The teacher may serve as the master of ceremonies or after the game is understood choose a student to fill that role.

Toss a coin to see which team will begin. The master of ceremonies describes the type of items included on this list. One at a time and without consultation, each participant of the beginning team suggests one item he/she believes will appear on the list. If the participant's response is correct, the strip of paper covering the item is removed before the next person on the team responds. For each incorrect response the scorekeeper marks a large "X" on the chalkboard. If the team records three incorrect responses, they lose their turn and the next team may attempt to finish the list.

A team scores 5 points when each person on the team responds and no more than two incorrect responses occurred. For example, on a 6-student team 5 points will be awarded if 4 or more items are correctly identified from the list. In the event that a team has 3 incorrect responses, the next team may attempt to complete the list. The second team receives credit for the items already correctly guessed by the first team. For example, if the first team (of 6 members) had correctly identified 2 items from the list before recording 3 incorrect responses, the second team only has to correctly identify 2 more items from the list to win the 5 points.

The winner may be the first team to win 25 points, or you may choose to set a time limit. Whoever is ahead at the end of the time limit wins.

Suggested List (with List Numbers):

Ten Oldest Colleges (14)
The Confederate States (31)
Flags Flown over Texas (41)
Nineteenth Century Authors (55)
Five-Star Generals (75)
Assassinated American Leaders (95)
Seven Wonders of the Ancient World (106)
The Axis Powers (143)
The Cabinet Positions (163)
Federal Legal Holidays (168)
Chief Justices of the Supreme Court (171)
Members of the Supreme Court (194)
Pioneers in the Field of Sociology (228)
Religious Symbols (246)
Words Borrowed from Spanish (250)
Southern Foods (254)

Things Not Around in 1960 (257)
Forms of American Music (259)
Major World Religions (264)
Ivy League Colleges (265)
Largest American Indian Tribes (276)
The Endocrine Glands (314)
Parts of the Brain (315)
The Continents (341)
The Provinces and Territories of
  of Canada (348)
Longest Rivers of the World (350)
The Great Lakes (360)
Soybean Products (369)
Major Wheat Producing Countries (371)

Cooperative Learning Reports

You can develop the attitudes and skills of cooperation by assigning small groups to work together on projects selected from the lists.

Preparation:

Select the list on which students will base their projects, for example, "Famous American Indians." Write each item on the list on a different piece of paper and place the slips in a box or sack.

Directions:

Break the class into cooperative learning groups of 2-4 students. (For more information on effectively developing cooperative learning groups, see D. W. Johnson and R. T. Johnson, *Learning Together and Alone* (Englewood Cliffs, NJ: Prentice Hall, 1987, or R. E. Slavin, *Cooperative Learning* (New York: Longman, 1983).) Each group draws a slip of paper selecting their topic for the project.

Describe the type of final product desired—written report, oral report, videotape, display, skit, etc. Encourage the groups to be creative in their approaches. Announce the final due date and if possible allot some class time for the groups to meet together to plan their projects.

Suggested Lists (with List Numbers):

Indian Tribes of the U.S. (1)
The Original American Colonies (2)
American Inventors (25)
Famous American Indians (28)
Major Civil War Battles (39)
Inventions of Thomas Edison (50)
The Muckrakers (56)
Fads and Fancies of the 1920's (65)
New Deal Programs (66)
Fads and Fancies of the 1930's (68)
Fads and Fancies of the 1950's (78)
Egyptian Deities (122)
Greek Gods and Goddesses (123)
Roman Deities (124)
The Bill of Rights (164)
Major Civil Rights Legislation (172)

Investment Opportunities (210)
American Architectural Styles (225)
U.S. Social Reformers (229)
Holy Books (247)
Contemporary Social Problems (253)
Major World Religions (264)
Eminent Pioneer Psychologists (284)
Counseling Approaches (287)
Common Defense Mechanisms (298)
Commonly Abused Drugs (308)
Provinces and Territories of Canada (348)
Major Crops of the United States (356)
Central American Countries & Capitals (374)
Countries & Capitals of Asia (375)
Countries and Capitals of Europe (377)

Scavenger Hunt

Arouse curiosity and encourage students to enter the room early by hiding items from one of the lists. This can be a fun way to introduce a new topic.

Preparation:

On separate 4" x 6" index cards, print individual items from one of the lists. Laminate the cards so they can be reused in future classes.

Directions:

Before students begin arriving for class, tape the cards around the room. Place them so they can be easily found, but in somewhat unusual spots (e.g., near the baseboard, on the wastebasket, beneath the pencil sharpener). Students should write down the items of the list as they discover them. It may stimulate enthusiasm to award a small prize or privilege to the person recording the most items from the list before class begins.

Suggested Lists (with List Numbers):

Indian Tribes (1)
North American Explorers (3)
Witticisms of Ben Franklin (10)
Achievements of Thomas Jefferson (18)
American Inventors (25)
Famous American Indians (28)
First Women (29)
Civil War Military Leaders (35)
Inventions of Thomas Edison (50)
Popular Songs of 1900 (52)
Woodrow Wilson's Fourteen Points (63)

Slang from the 1920's (64)
Foods & Fancies of 1920's (65)
American Automobiles of the 1920's (69)
Slang of the 1960's (82)
Nicknames of Famous Americans (97)
Ancient Units of Measurement (111)
"Love" in Many Languages (130)
Original Members of the United Nations (148)
The Cabinet Offices (163)
Portraits on U.S. Currency (169)

The Federal Reserve Banks (173)
Home Fire Hazards (219)
Labor Unions (220)
Folk Medicines (232)
Cowboy Slang (235)
Wedding Customs (240)
The Golden Rule in Many Religions (245)
Words Borrowed From African
  Languages (249)
Australian Slang (251)
Forms of American Music (259)
Advice from Aesop (263)
Major World Religions (264)
Phobias (286)

Common Defense Mechanisms (298)
The Most Common Fears (307)
Time Management Strategies (328)
Hearing Impaired Persons of Note (333)
Current Names of Old Places (337)
Nicknames of the States (345)
The 20 Most Populous Countries (349)
Weather Signs From American
  Folklore (352)
Largest Islands (363)
Geographic Nicknames (367)
Major Petroleum Producing
  Countries (372)
World's Largest Cities (378)

Pairing Puzzles

This is a fun way to break the class into pairs.

Preparation:

Select a list which offers pairs of items such as vocabulary, nicknames, or achievements. Print the pairs on a sheet of paper as a matching quiz (for example, writing the names of inventors on the left and their invention on the right half). Cut each card in half such that they key word (inventors) and its match (invention) are on separate halves. Use a zigzag cut so that no two halves will be exactly the same. Shuffle the half pages sheets to mix up the order. There should be a sufficient number of cards for each pair of students.

Directions:

Distribute the cut card so that each student ends up with one half. Students must mingle to locate the student with the piece which matches their half. In pairs, students may now complete activities such as the Matching Game or Cooperative Learning Reports. If you have an odd number of students, include one "wild card." That student becomes a third member of a selected group. You may let the student choose which pair to join, or you may select it.

Suggested Lists (with List Numbers):

Nicknames of the Presidents (6)
U.S. Women's First (29)
Slang of the 1920's (64)
Slang of the 1930's (67)
Slang of the 1950's (77)
Slang of the 1960's (82)
Nicknames of Famous Americans (97)
Nicknames of Various World Leaders (118)
Fathers of . . . (120)
Egyptian Dieties (122)
"Hello" in Many Languages (128)
"Love" in Many Languages (130)

The Cabinet Offices (163)
Portraits on U.S. Currency (169)
Household Measures (205)
Esperanto Vocabulary (233)
Cowboy Slang (235)
Australian Slang (251)
Phobias (286)
Counseling Approaches (287)
Current Names of Old Places (337)
Nicknames of the States (345)
Countries & Capitals of South
  America (373)
Countries & Capitals of Africa (376)

Press Conferences

Get students personally involved in social studies content and encourage listening skills with simulated press interviews.

Preparation:

Select an appropriate list related to a topic the class will be studying. Lists of names work best for this activity. Type each item from the list on separate sheets and mix in a box or hat.

Directions:

Allow each student to draw a card from the box or hat. They are assigned to research that person. Allow at least a week for the research. Encourage students to enmesh themselves into the lives of the persons they are studying, to learn as much as they can about that character and the world in which he/she lived. On the due date(s) individuals are interviewed by the "press corps," which might be a selected group of 4-5 students. The format is much like that of a presidential news conference. Rotate interviewers as each new person is interviewed. As an option, students may be encouraged to dress as their "character." Interviews might be spread out over several weeks. This activity may be used as an extra credit option.

Suggested Lists (with List Numbers):

Patriot Leaders of the American
  Revolution (11)
American Inventors (25)
Major American Indian Leaders (27)
Famous Native American Indians (28)
First Women (29)
Civil War Military Leaders (35)
Famous Outlaws of the West (45)
The Muckrakers (56)
Women's Rights Pioneers (57)
Labor Leaders (59)
Nicknames of Famous Americans (97)

Nicknames of Famous World Leaders
  (118)
Fathers of . . . (120)
Nobel Peace Prize Winners of the
  1980's (157)
The Cabinet Offices (163)
Chief Justices of the Supreme Court
  (171)
Civil Rights Leaders (192)
U.S. Social Reformers (229)
Ten Largest American Indian Tribes
  (276)
Counseling Approaches (287)

Brainstorming

Encourage cooperation and develop listening skills through small group brainstorming. This is also an effective technique for introducing a new topic.

Preparation:

Minimal preparation is required beyond selection of the appropriate list.

Directions:

Divide the class into small groups of 4-5 persons. Identify a leader for each group. A fun way to select leaders is to ask for each group to determine who got up earliest that morning or who has the most brothers and sisters. The leader's role is to keep everyone on task and to record the group's answers. For variety, large group brainstorming can be done with the entire class. Select two students to write the list on the board as items are suggested.

If the students are not familiar with brainstorming, explain that the focus is upon quantity, to name as many items as they can which belong to the selected list. Allow a maximum of five minutes for the brainstorming session. Have each group in turn share two items from their list until all are mentioned. Reveal the total list on a transparency or handout, or just read the ones that have not been mentioned by the students.

Suggested Lists (with List Numbers):

Indian Tribes of the United States (1)
The Original American Colonies (2)
North American Explorers (3)
Revolutionary War Battles (13)
Ten Oldest Colleges (14)
Largest Cities in 1790 (15)
Famous American Indiana (28)
The Confederate States (31)
Civil War Military Leaders (35)
Major Civil War Battles (39)
Automobiles of the 1930's (69)
Wars Involving the United States (89)
The Seven Wonders of the Ancient World (106)

Greek Gods and Goddesses (123)
Major Roman Deities (124)
Signs of the Zodiac (134)
The Axis Powers (143)
The Cabinet Offices (163)
The Bill of Rights (164)
Federal Legal Holidays (168)
Home Fire Hazards (219)
Labor Unions (220)
Commonly Abused Drugs (308)
Provinces and Territories of Canada (348)

Bingo

You'll be surprised how much students remember when lists are incorporated into versions of BINGO. This can be an effective technique for emphasizing the breadth of a list, such as contributions by women, or the variety of American Indian tribes. It is a fun way to introduce a new topic.

Preparation:

The easiest way to make the game cards is to duplicate the blank BINGO card on the following page. Give each student a copy or write the selected list on the chalkboard. The lists used should have at least 24 items. Have the students fill the 24 open boxes in their BINGO cards with separate items from the list. They should mix up the order of the items as they write so that no two cards will be exactly the same. You will also need about 20 beans or pieces of corn for student.

Cut up a copy of the list so that each item of the list is on a separate slip of paper. Be sure each item on the list is included. Place all slips in a box or sack and shake up. You may choose to laminate and save the game cards for use with future classes.

Directions:

When each student has a game card with items of the list written in the open boxes, the game is ready to begin. It is played much like the traditional game of BINGO. As a slip is drawn from the box, it is read aloud. Each student who has that item on his/her card places a bean or kernel of corn on that box. The winner is the first person to get five items in a row vertically, horizontally, or diagonally. Everyone begins with the center box covered as a free one. A winner calls out "Bingo." It is probably a good idea to verify that the person does indeed have five in a row.

To build enthusiasm for the game, award a small prize to the winners. It can be a classroom privilege, small token, poster, button, free sports tickets, or other freebie.

Suggested Lists (with List Numbers):

Indian Tribes of the United States (1)

American Inventors (25)

Major American Indian Leaders (27)

U.S. Women's Firsts (29)

Civil War Military Leaders (35)

Major Civil War Battles (39)

Slang of the 1920's (64)

Fads and Fancies of the 1950's (78)

The Greek Alphabet (119)

"Peace" in Many Languages (129)

Original Members of the United Nations (148)

Home Fire Safety Checklist (219)

Notable Hispanic Americans (255)

Forms of American Music (259)

Phobias (286)

Counseling Approaches (287)

Feelings (306)

Nicknames of the States (345)

Soybean Products (369)

Countries & Capitals of Africa (376)

B I N G O

		FREE		

Matching Quiz

Stimulate interest by having pairs of students attempt to match pairs of items from lists.

Preparation:

Select a list which offers pairs of items such as vocabulary, nicknames, or achievements. Print or type the list on a sheet of paper as a matching quiz, for example, listing names in the left-hand column and in scrambled order their accomplishments in the right-hand column. Duplicate a sufficient number for each pair of students.

Directions:

Form pairs either at random or using a technique such as Puzzle Pairing. Distribute a quiz sheet to each pair. Direct the students to connect each item from the left-hand list to the appropriate item on the right-hand list with a straight line. After 3-5 minutes, call time and score the results.

Suggested Lists (with List Numbers):

Nicknames of the Presidents (6)
U.S. Women's Firsts (29)
Slang of the 1920's (64)
Slang of the 1930's (67)
Slang of the 1950's (77)
Slang of the 1960's (82)
Nicknames of Famous Americans (97)
Fathers of . . . (120)
Egyptian Dieties (122)
"Hello" in Many Languages (128)
"Peace" in Many Languages (129)
The Cabinet Offices (163)

Portraits on U.S. Currency (169)
Household Measures (205)
Esperanto Vocabulary (233)
Cowboy Slang (235)
Phobias (286)
Current Names of Old Places (337)
Nicknames of the States (345)
Countries & Capitals of South
    America (373)
Countries & Capitals of Asia (375)
Countries & Capitals of Europe (377)
Counseling Approaches (387)

Crossword Puzzles

Spark interest or review through crossword puzzles based on appropriate lists. An example based on List 345, "Nicknames of the States," is presented on the following page.

Preparation:

Using an appropriate list, construct a crossword puzzle. A very useful computer program, "Crossword Magic," is available for the Apple GS or Macintosh computers from Mindscape, Inc., 3444 Dundee Road, Northbrook, IL 60062, or most major computer software mail-order houses. You may choose to give the students a list including the words used in the puzzle. Duplicate copies of the finished puzzle. You might challenge older students to construct their own puzzles.

Directions:

Distribute a copy of the puzzle for each student or to each pair. Crossword puzzles can be completed in pairs, in class or as homework. It is generally best to permit students to use whatever resources they can as this reinforces information-gathering skills. Post the answers.

Nicknames of the States

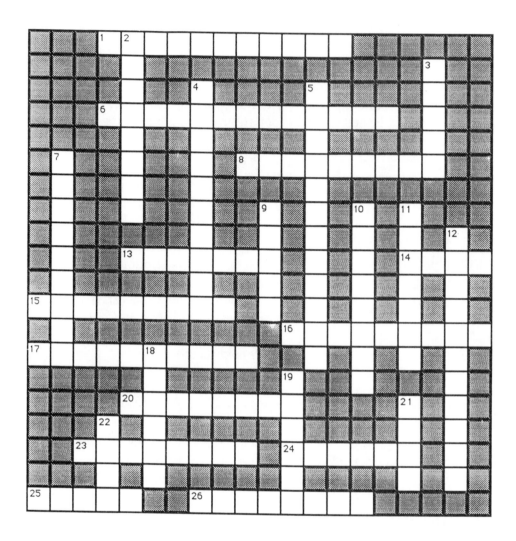

Across
1. Nutmeg State
6. Bay State
8. Volunteer State
13. Big Sky Country
14. Buckeye State
15. Bayou State
16. Badger State
17. Golden State
20. Diamond State
23. Centennial State
24. Land of the Midnight Sun
25. Lone Star State
26. Cornhusker State

Down
2. Sooner State
3. Pine Tree State
4. Evergreen State
5. Keystone State
7. Gopher State
9. Gem State
10. Bluegrass State
11. Cowboy State
12. Magnolia State
18. Beaver State
19. Silver State
21. Beehive State
22. Hawkeye State

Suggested Lists (with List Numbers):

Foods of the Colonial Era (5)
Nicknames of the Presidents (6)
Revolutionary War Battles (13)
Earliest Colleges (14)
Tools of the Pioneers (21)
American Inventors (25)
Famous American Indians (28)
U.S. Women's Firsts (29)
The Confederate States (31)
Civil War Military Leaders (35)
Major Civil War Battles (39)
Infamous Outlaws of the West (45)
Sailing Vessels (47)
The Muckrakers (56)
Labor Leaders (59)
Slang from the 1920's (64)
Nicknames of Famous Americans (97)
Major Egyptian Dieties (122)

Greek Dieties (123)
Roman Dieties (124)
The Cabinet Offices (163)
The Bill of Rights (164)
Portraits on U.S. Currency (169)
Military Ranks (177)
Personal Assets (216)
Counseling Approaches (287)
Common Defense Mechanisms (298)
Current Names of Old Places (337)
The Provinces and Territories of
  Canada (348)
Farm Animals (357)
Largest Islands (363)
Geographic Nicknames (367)
Central American Countries &
  Capitals (374)
Countries & Capitals of Asia (375)
Countries & Capitals of Africa (376)

Anagrams

Anagrams, or words with the letters scrambled, can be used to develop interest in a topic and to practice problem-solving skills.

Preparation:

Select a list comprised of one-word items. On a chalkboard, newsprint, or handout, rearrange the letters of the words on the list using all capital letters. For example, from the list of the states the anagram KASALA would unscramble ALASKA. A maximum of ten words is sufficient for all but the more advanced classes.

Directions:

Reveal or distribute the anagrams. Tell the students the topic of the lists (e.g., States of the Union). While the puzzles can be done individually either in class or as homework, it is probably best to randomly pair students. This encourages cooperation and minimizes the disadvantages of ability. If spelling may be a problem, a copy of the correctly spelled list might be posted. Anagrams may also be distributed as "fillers" to constructively occupy idle moments such as when students complete a list early.

Suggested Lists (with List Numbers):

Indian Tribes of the United States (1)
North American Explorers (3)
Tools of the Pioneers (21)
Famous American Indians (28)
Weaponry of the Civil War (36)

Signs of the Zodiac (134)
The Axis Powers (143)
The Cabinet Offices (163)
Military Ranks (177)
The Presidents (178)

Dictionary Game

This is a variation of the old party game. The idea of the game is to guess the correct definition of an unfamiliar word. It works well with lists which include words which are entirely new to the students. You will need a sufficient supply of identical 3" x 5" cards or pieces of paper for each student to have six pieces.

Preparation:

Advance preparation consists of selecting a list related to the topic the class is studying. It is important that the students are unlikely to know the words on the list. For each item on the list, write the word and its definition on a card or paper. You will need one set of cards for every five students in the class.

Directions:

Break the class into groups of five or six students and have them gather in small circles. Each student will need the same number of cards as there are in the prepared deck. Place a set of prepared cards face down in the center of each group. One student begins by selecting at random one card from the deck and reading aloud the word from the card, but not its definition. The task is for each student to then make up a plausible definition and write it on one of their cards. They should not see each other's definitions. If they should know the real definition, they should not tell anyone and make up a phoney one. Encourage them to print neatly so that the definition can be easily read.

The cards are then given to the student who drew the original card. He or she will shuffle the cards, including the original one, and then read aloud all the definitions. After all the definitions have been read, the other students are to vote on which they believe is the correct one. Each time they guess correctly they receive one point.

Rotating clockwise around the circle the process is repeated until all the cards in the deck have been used.

Suggested Lists (with List Numbers):

Slang of the 1890's (48)   "Hello" in Many Languages (128)
Slang of the 1920's (64)   "Peace" in Many Languages (129)
Slang of the 1930's (67)   "Love" in Many Languages (130)
Slang of the 1940's (71)   Esperanto Vocabulary (233)
Slang of the 1950's (77)   Cowboy Slang (235)
Slang of the 1960's (82)   Australian Slang (251)
Slang of the 1970's (93)   Phobias (286)

Interest Builders

Posters

Design (or let students make) colorful posters which incorporate the lists. Add pictures, drawings, and designs related to the theme of the list. The posters can be displayed on the door or in the room as interest grabbers. Try hanging a new one each day or on random days. The element of surprise gets student's attention. They begin to read the posters before class begins. Save them for use next year.

Bulletin Board Displays

Challenge a group of students to design and construct an attractive bulletin board display (either in the classroom or in a hallway) which incorporates one of the lists. Photos, drawings, and color add to the interest.

Coming Attractions

As a homework assignment announce the topic of one of the lists (e.g., Items Rationed During World War II (76), Common Superstitions (312), Southern Foods (254), or Folk Medicines (232)). Have the students enlist the aid of their parents in listing as many items as they can. In the next class, have students call out their items as one student records them on the board. Add any from the published list that are not mentioned by the students.

Learning Centers

Incorporate lists into learning centers. Photos or drawings which illustrate the lists will add interest. The goal should not be to memorize the lists, but rather to use them to reinforce a concept, apply a skill, challenge assumptions, develop appreciation, or influence attitudes.

Handouts

Some of the lists make useful handouts which the students can read and take home. They will not only arouse students' interest but parents' as well.

Overhead Transparencies

Include some of the lists on overhead transparencies. Turn on the transparency before the class begins. Students who arrive early can enjoy the day's list. When the bell rings, turn off the transparency. This rewards students who are on time and increases the day's learning time, as well as arousing interest in the day's topic. If time permits at the end of class, you may put the transparency back on.

Section I

LISTS FOR
UNITED STATES
HISTORY

1. Early Indian Tribes of the U.S.

Apache
Arapaho
Caddo
Catawba
Cayuga
Cherokee
Cheyenne
Chickasaw
Chippewa
Choctaw
Commanche
Creek
Delaware
Herring Pond
Illinois
Iowa
Iroquois
Kansa
Kaskaskia
Kickapoo
Kiowa Apache
Mattaponi
Menomenee
Miami
Mohican
Munsee
Narragansett
Nottaway

Oneida
Onondaga
Osage
Oto
Ottawa
Pamunkey
Passamaquoddy
Pawnee
Penobscot
Peoria
Piankashaw
Ponco
Potawatomie
Quapuw
Sac
Saulk
Seminole
Seneca
Shawnee
Sopoonee
Tonkawa
Tuscarora
Wampanoag
Wichita
Winnebago
Wisconsin
Wyandot
Yuchi

2. Original American Colonies

Colony	Date settled
Virginia	1607
Plymouth	1620
Maine & New Hampshire	1622
Massachusetts	1630
Maryland	1634
Connecticut	1636
Rhode Island	1636
Delaware	1638
North Carolina	1653
New York	1664
New Jersey	1664
South Carolina	1670
Pennsylvania	1681
Georgia	1733

3. North American Explorers

(see also List 137, "Early Explorers of the Americas")
James Bridger
Samuel de Champlain
William Clark
John C. Fremont
Henry Hudson
Louis Jolliet
Sieur de La Salle
Meriwether Lewis
Jacques Marquette
Zebulon Pike

4. Major Documents in American History

Mayflower Compact, 1620
Declaration of Independence, 1776
Articles of Confederation, 1781
Northwest Ordinance, 1787
Constitution, 1787
Emancipation Proclamation, 1863
Atlantic Charter, 1941

5. Foods of Colonial Americans

apples
beans
berries
carrots
cheese
chickens
cider
cornbread
corn fritters
dumplings
fish
grapes
hoecake
hominy
honey
johnnycake
maize (Indian corn)
maple sugar
mush
oysters
pears
peas
popcorn
pork
porridge
pumpkin
salt
shoofly pie
squash
stews
succotash
tea
turnips
wild game
wild plums
wine

6. Nicknames of the Presidents

George Washington	Father of His Country; The Sage of Mt. Vernon
John Adams	The Atlas of Independence, Bonny Johnny, His Rotundity
Thomas Jefferson	Apostle of Democracy, Long Tom, The Pen of the Revolution
James Madison	Father of the Constitution, Little Johnny, Sage of Montpelier
James Monroe	The Last of the Cocked Hats
John Quincy Adams	Old Man Eloquent, Publicola
Andrew Jackson	Old Hickory, The Old Hero, King Andrew the First
Martin Van Buren	The Red Fox of Kinderbrook, The Little Magician, Little Van
William Henry Harrison	Old Tippecanoe, The Cincinnatus of the West, Old Granny
John Tyler	His Accidency, Young Hickory
James K. Polk	Polk the Purposeful, Napoleon of the Stump
Zachary Taylor	Old Rough and Ready, Old Zack
Millard Fillmore	The Accidental President, The Wool Carder President
Franklin Pierce	Handsome Frank, Purse
James Buchanan	Old Buck, The Do-Nothing President
Abraham Lincoln	The Great Emancipator, Honest Abe, The Rail Splitter
Andrew Johnson	The Tailor, Sir Veto, Father of the Homestead Act
Ulysses S. Grant	American Caesar, The Galena Tanner, Useless Grant
Rutherford B. Hayes	His Fraudulency, Old 8 to 7
James A. Garfield	The Canal Boy, The Preacher President
Chester A. Arthur	
Grover Cleveland	Grover the Good, Old Grover
Benjamin Harrison	Young Tippecanoe, Little Ben, The Centennial President
William McKinley	Liberator of Cuba, The Idol of Ohio, Wobbly Willie
Theodore Roosevelt	The Rough Rider, The Cowboy President, T.R.
William H. Taft	
Woodrow Wilson	The Professor, The Phrasemaker
William G. Harding	W.G.
Calvin Coolidge	Silent Cal
Herbert Hoover	Chief, Grand Old Man
Franklin D. Roosevelt	F.D.R., The Boss, King Franklin
Harry S. Truman	Give 'em Hell Harry, Haberdasher Harry
Dwight D. Eisenhower	General Ike, Kansas Cyclone, Duckpin
John F. Kennedy	J.F.K.
Lyndon B. Johnson	L.B.J.
Richard M. Nixon	Tricky Dick, Richard the Chicken-Hearted
Gerald Ford	Jerry
Jimmy Carter	The Peanut Farmer, Cousin Hot
Ronald Reagan	The Great Communicator, Dutch, Ronald the Right
George Bush	

7. Parts of a Revolutionary War General's Uniform

boots
coat skirt
crossbelt
epaulette
frock coat
gloves
knee britches
infantry button
scabbard
sword
tricorn
waistcoat

8. Famous Americans Who Also Taught School

John Adams	U.S. President
Louisa May Alcott	author
Chester A. Arthur	U.S. President
Clara Barton	Founder of American Red Cross
Alexander Graham Bell	inventor
Dan Blocker	"Hoss" from *Bonanza*
Clarence Darrow	attorney
Amelia Earhart	aviator
Geraldine Ferraro	vice presidential candidate
Roberta Flack	singer
Abigail Fillmore	First Lady
Margaret Fuller	transcendentalist author; social reformer
Art Garfunkel	singer
John Wesley Hardin	outlaw
Janis Joplin	rock star
Lyndon B. Johnson	U.S. President
William McKinley	U.S. President
Anne Murray	singer
Carry Nation	temperance leader
Pat Nixon	First Lady
Thomas Paine	colonial patriot
Gen. John Pershing	chief of World War I American Expeditionary Force
Dixie Lee Ray	governor of Washington
Eleanor Roosevelt	First Lady, author, lecturer
Gene Simmons	member of rock group "KISS"
Margaret Chase Smith	U.S. Senator from Maine
William Quantrill	Confederate guerilla leader
Mary Church Terrell	social reformer

9. Contributions of Ben Franklin

Clerk of the Philadelphia Assembly
Editor of *Pennsylvania Gazette*
Published *Poor Richard's Almanack*
First editor in America to publish a newspaper cartoon
First editor in America to use maps to illustrate news stories
Postmaster of *Philadelphia Deputy*
First proposed daylight savings time
Established first city mail delivery
Established first subscription library
Organized Philadelphia fire department
Raised money to build Pennsylvania Hospital in Philadelphia
Helped found academy which became University of Pennsylvania
Electrical experiment that proved that lightning was electricity
Discovered that diseases spread rapidly in poorly ventilated rooms
Invented lightning rod
Invented bifocal glasses
Invented the Franklin stove
Unofficial ambassador to England
Invented the rocking chair
Elected to Second Continental Congress
Organzied national post office
Minister to France
Helped write the Treaty of Paris
President of the Executive Council of Pennsylvania
Delegate to the Constitutional Convention
President of America's first anti-slavery society

10. Witticisms of Ben Franklin

"Early to bed and early to rise, makes a man healthy, wealthy, and wise."

"God helps them that help themselves."

"Little strokes fell great oaks."

"He that falls in love with himself will have no rivals."

"An ounce of prevention is worth a pound of cure."

"He's a fool that makes his doctor heir."

"Eat to live and not live to eat."

"Three may keep a secret if two of them are dead."

"Lost time is never found again."

"Remember that time is money."

"There never was a good war or a bad peace."

"Don't throw stones at neighbors if your own windows are glass."

"We must all hang together, or most assuredly, we shall hang separately."

"Fish and visitors stink after three days."

"You may delay, but time will not."

"Be slow in choosing a friend, slower in changing."

"There is no little enemy."

"He that lives upon hope will die fasting."

"They that can give up essential liberty to obtain a little temporary safety deserve neither liberty nor safety."

"I shall never ask, never refuse, not ever resign an office."

"Sin is not hurtful because it is forbidden, but it is forbidden because it is hurtful."

"Sell not virtue to purchase wealth, not liberty to purchase power."

"Laws gentle are seldom obeyed; too severe seldom executed."

"Our Constitution is in actual operation; everything appears to promise that it will last; but nothing in this world is certain but death and taxes."

11. Patriot Leaders of the American Revolution

John Adams
Samuel Adams
Silas Deane
Benjamin Franklin
John Hancock
Patrick Henry
John Jay
Thomas Jefferson
Richard Henry Lee
Robert Livingston
George Mason
Robert Morris
James Otis
Thomas Paine
Paul Revere
George Washington

12. American Military Leaders of the Revoutionary War

Ethan Allen
Benedict Arnold
George R. Clark
George Clinton
Horatio Gates
Nathanael Greene
Nathan Hale
John Paul Jones
Henry Knox
Charles Lee
Henry Lee
Francis Marion
Rufus Putnam
Arthur St. Clair
Philip Schuyler
Artemas Ward
Seth Warner
George Washington
Anthony Wayne

13. Revolutionary War Battles

1775

Apr. 19	Lexington & Concord	Massachusetts
June 17	Bunker Hill	Massachusetts
Nov. 13	Montreal	Quebec
Dec. 31	Quebec	Quebec

1776

Aug. 27	Long Island	New York
Dec. 26	Trenton	New Jersey

1777

Jan. 3	Princeton	New Jersey
Aug. 16	Bennington	Vermont/New York
Sept. 11	Brandywine	Pennsylvania
Sept. 19	Freeman's Farm	New York
Oct. 4	Germantown	Pennsylvania
Oct. 7	Freeman's Farm	New York

1778

June 28	Monmouth	New Jersey

1779

Sept. 23	*Bonhomme Richard* vs. *Serapis*	North Sea

1780

Aug. 16	Camden	South Carolina
Oct. 7	Kings Mountain	South Carolina

1781

Mar. 15	Guilford Courthouse	North Carolina
Oct. 6-19	Yorktown	Virginia

14. Earliest Colleges

College	Founded	Location
Harvard College	1636	Cambridge, MA
William and Mary	1693	Williamsburg, VA
Yale	1700	New Haven, CT
New Jersey	1746	Princeton, NJ
Washington & Lee	1749	Lexington, VA
Kings (Columbia)	1754	New York
Philadelphia (Univ. of Pennsylvania)	1755	Philadelphia
Rhode Island College (Brown)	1764	Providence
Queen's College (Rutgers)	1766	New Brunswick, NJ
Dartmouth	1769	Hanover, NH

15. Largest U.S. Cities in 1790

Philadelphia	42,444
New York	33,131
Boston	18,038
Charlestown	16,359
Baltimore	13,503
Salem	7,921
Newport	6,716

Source: Bureau of the Census

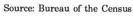

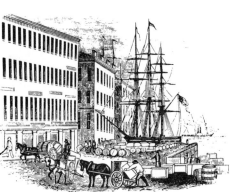

16. 1790 Slave Population

New Hampshire	157
Rhode Island	958
Connecticut	2,648
New York	21,193
New Jersey	11,423
Pennsylvania	3,707
Delaware	8,887
Maryland	103,036
Virginia	292,627
North Carolina	100,783
South Carolina	107,094
Georgia	29,264
Kentucky	12,430
Southwest Territory	3,417
UNITED STATES	697,624

Source: Bureau of the Census

17. Major Events of 1800

Library of Congress was established.
Land Act of 1800 spurred land speculation.
President John Adams fired Secretary of State, Thomas Pickering.
Slave insurrection in Virginia thwarted; leader, Gabriel, hanged.
Congress moved to Washington, new national capital.
The Evangelical Church was founded.
Presidential campaign between John Adams, Federalist, and Thomas Jeffer-
    son, Democratic-Republican, resulted in electoral college tie.
Santee Canal in South Carolina was completed.
Second U.S. census was conducted.
The Federalist Party held the first secret congressional caucus.
First vaccination for smallpox was administered by Benjamin Waterhouse.
Sailors went on strike in New York City.
Eli Whitney made muskets with interchangeable parts.
The first book with color plates was printed.
New York City equipped the first fireboat to be used in the United States.

18. Achievements of Thomas Jefferson

Served in the Virginia House of Burgess
Wrote the Declaration of Independence
Elected governor of Virginia
Served as minister to France
Secretary of State
Vice President of the United States
President of the United States
Orchestrated the Louisiana Purchase
Founded University of Virginia
Designed his mountaintop home, Monticello

19. Battles of the War of 1812

1812
Queenston Heights
1813
Lake Erie
Thames River
1814
Raisin River Massacre
Lake Champlain
Lundy's Lane
1815
New Orleans

20. Early Firearms

blunderbuss
Colt Peacemaker
derringer
dueling pistols
flintlock
Kentucky long rifle
matchlock
percussion rifle
Remington revolver
wheellock pistol

21. Tools of the Pioneers

adze
anvil
auger
axe
barrels
bellows
branding iron
broad axe
buck saw
corn knife
corn planter
crosscut saw
drawknife
flail
forge
froe
grain cradle
grindstone
hammer
hand cultivator
harrow
hatchet
hoe

hog scraper
hoof files
knives
mallet
mattock
maul
oxen yoke
pick
pitchfork
plane
potato digger
rake
sack needles
saddles
scythe
shovel
sickle
spoke shavers
wedges
whetstone

22. Household Implements of the Pioneers

apple peeler
bean pot
bed warmer
butter churn
butter mold
candle mold
candle snuffer
cider press
copper kettles
corn grater
crocks
fire screen
flat iron
foot stove
iron cooking pot
kettles
ladles
lard press
loom
milk strainer
quilting frame
razor strop
sausage gun
sieves
skin stretchers
spinning wheel
splint broom
tinderbox
washboard
whale oil lamp
wooden buckets
wooden trencher & spoons

23. Percentage of Slaveowners, 1850

State	Percent of total white population
New England	
Maine	0
New Hampshire	0
Vermont	0
Massachusetts	0
Rhode Island	0
Middle States	
New York	0
New Jersey	0.2
Pennsylvania	0
Delaware	6.5
Southern States	
Maryland & District of Columbia	21.9
Virginia	35.1
North Carolina	29.2
South Carolina	53.1
Georgia	42.0
Florida	42.5
Kentucky	28.7
Tennessee	25.5
Alabama	39.2
Mississippi	44.6
Louisiana	46.1
Texas	28.7
Arkansas	21.1
Missouri	18.5
United States	10.1

Source: U.S. Census Bureau. *A Century of Population Growth*. Washington, D.C.: Government Printing Office, 1909.

24. Firsts of the 1850's

The following pioneering efforts all occurred during the 1850's:

First female college graduate, Oberlin College
Private railroad car used by Jenny Lind
School for mentally retarded opened, Boston
National Women's Rights Convention
Condensed milk produced
YMCA organized in Boston
Stereoscope invented
College to prevent discrimination in race, color or creed, Cooper Union
Safety elevator manufactured
Commercial oil well drilled at Titusville, Pennsylvania
Oil refinery constructed
Compulsory school attendance law enacted, Massachusetts
Railroad suspension bridge built
Veterinary school founded, Boston
Woman's college founded, Elmira, New York
Discovery of borax
Gold used in dental fillings
Trans-Atlantic cable laid
School band formed
Toilet paper manufactured
College for blacks founded, Chester County, Pennsylvania
School for the blind formed in St. Louis
Rotary washing machine manufactured
Electric stove invented
Railroads expand west of the Mississippi
Cable street car invented
Roll-top desk manufactured
Intercollegiate baseball game
Typesetting machine built
Pencil with attached eraser manufactured
Bloomers introduced
Braille taught to blind students
U.S. Navy bans flogging
United States population surpasses 25 million
New York Times begins publication
Walter Hunt patents disposable paper collar
U.S. Army buys pack camels for the desert southwest
Mardi Gras parades held in New Orleans
California, Oregon and Minnesota are admitted as states
Cast iron frame building constructed
Longfellow writes "The Song of Hiawatha"
Perry negotiates first American-Japanese treaty
First spinal anesthesia used by J.L. Corning

25. American Inventors & Their Inventions

Invention	Inventor	Year
Lightning rod	Benjamin Franklin	1752
Bifocal glasses	Benjamin Franklin	c. 1760
Steam boat	John Fitch	1787
Cotton gin	Eli Whitney	1793
Cotton sewing thread	Mrs. Samuel Slater	1793
Comb cutting machine	Phineas Pratt	1799
Aerosol spray gun	Alan de Vilbiss	1803
Screw propellor	John Stevens	1804
Reaper	Cyrus McCormick	1834
Threshing machine	Hiram and John Pitts	1834
Revolver	Samuel Colt	1835
Morse code	S. B. Morse	1836
Steel plow	John Deere	1837
Rubber vulcanization	Charles Goodyear	1839
Life preserver	Napoleon Guerin	1841
Sewing machine	Elias Howe	1846
Commercial chewing gum	John Bacon Curtis	1848
Baby carriage	Charles Burton	1848
Safety pin	Walter Hunt	1849
Device to buoy vessels over shoals	Abraham Lincoln	1849
Roll-top desk	Abner Cutler	1850
Bloomers	Amelia Bloomer, E. Smith	1851
Cylinder lock	Linus Yale, Jr.	1851
Safety elevator	Elisha Otis	1854
Accordian	Anthony Faas	1854
Calliope	Joshua Stoddard	1855
Machine gun	Charles Barnes	1856
Mason jar	J. Mason	1858
Cable car	Eleazer Gardner	1858
Paper dress patterns	Eleanor Butterick	1863
Sleeping car	George M. Pullman	1865
Typewriter	Christopher Sholes	1867
Air brake	George Westinghouse	1868
Plywood	John Mayo	1868
Brown paper bags	Margaret Knight	1870
Stock ticker	Thomas Edison	1870
Gasoline engine	George Brayton	1872
Jeans	Oscar Levi Strauss	1873
Barbed wire	Joseph Glidden	1874
Telephone	Alexander Graham Bell	1876
Carpet sweeper	Melville Bissell	1876
Mimeograph	Thomas Edison	1876
Phonograph	Thomas Edison	1877
Catamaran	Nathaneal Herreschoff	1877

25. American Inventors & Their Inventions, continued

Invention	Inventor	Year
Incandescent lamp	Thomas Edison	1879
Cash register	John Ritty	1879
Electric fan	Schuyler Wheeler	1882
Fountain pen	Lewis Waterman	1884
Roller skate	Levant Richardson	1884
Adding machine	William Burroughs	1885
Linotype	Ottmar Mergenthaler	1885
Motorcycle	Gottlieb Daimler	1885
Coca-Cola®	John S. Pemberton	1886
Kodak box camera	George Eastman	1888
Ballpoint pen	John H. Land	1888
Pneumatic hammer	Charles King	1890
Submarine	John P. Holland	1891
Zipper	Whitcomb Judson	1893
Movie machine	Thomas Edison	1893
Corn flakes	John H. Kellogg	1894
Safety razor	King C. Gillette	1895
Electric stove	William Hadaway	1896
Pencil sharpener	J.L. Love	1897
Golf tee	George Grant	1899
Tractor	Benjamin Holt	1900
Mouse trap	Charles Nelson	1900
Hair straightener	Sarah Breedlove Walker	1905
Radio amplifier	Lee De Forest	1907
Electric vacuum cleaner	Spangler	1907
Kewpie doll	Rose O'Neill	1907
Drip coffee	Melitta Bentz	1908
Electric auto starter	Charles Kettering	1911
Air conditioning	Willis Carrier	1911
Crossword puzzle	Arthur Wynne	1913
Vacuum cleaner	James Kirby	1916
Arc welder	Thomson	1919
Lie detector	John Larsen	1921
Talking movie	Warner brothers	1927
Snowmobile	Carl Eliason	1927
Iron lung	Lewis Slaw & Phillip Drinker	1928
Rocket engine	Robert H. Goddard	1929
Analog computer	Vannevar Bush	1930
Electric razor	Jacob Schick	1931
Cyclotron	Ernest O. Lawrence	1931
Chocolate chip cookie	Ruth Wakefield	1933
Launderette	Cantrell	1934
Nylon	Edwin Armstrong	1935
Parking meter	Carlton Magee	1935
Xerography	Chester Carlson	1938

25. American Inventors & Their Inventions, continued

Invention	Inventor	Year
Helicopter	Igor Ivan Sikorsky	1939
Radar	Robert Page	1940
Polaroid camera	Edwin H. Land	1947
Long playing record	Goldmark	1947
Microwave oven	Percy LeBaron Spencer	1947
Transistor	John Bardeen	1948
Disposable diaper	Marion Donovan	1950
Computer compiler	Grace Murray Hopper	1952
Panoramic movie	Waller	1952
Polio vaccine	Jonas Salk	1953
Heart-lung machine	John Gibbon	1953
Calculator	George Stibitz	1954
Liquid Paper®	Belle Nesmith Graham	1956
Barbie doll	Ruth Handler	1959
Integrated circuit	Jack S. Kilby	1959
Laser	Theodore Maiman	1960
Music synthesizer	Robert A. Moog	1964
Noise reduction system	Ray Dolby	1966
Solar powered aircraft	Paul Macready	1980
Artificial heart	Robert Jarvik	1982

26. The Transcendentalists

Bronson Alcott

Orestes A. Brownson

Emily Dickinson

Ralph Waldo Emerson

Margaret Fuller

Nathaniel Hawthorne

Fredric Hedge

Joseph Palmer

Theodore Parker

Elizabeth Palmer Peabody

George Ripley

Henry David Thoreau

27. Major American Indian Leaders

Leader	Lifespan	Tribe
American Horse	1801-1876	Ogala Sioux
Attakullakulla	1700?-1778	Cherokee
Big Bear	1825-1888	Plains Cree
Big Foot	1825-1890	Sioux
Black Elk	1863-1950	Ogala Sioux
Black Hawk	1767?-1838	Sac
Black Kettle	1803-1868	Cheyenne
Joseph Brant	1742-1807	Mohawk
Captain Jack	1840-1873	Modac
Chato	1860-1934	Chiricahua
Cochise	1812?-1874	Apache
Cornplanter	1735?-1836	Seneca
Crazy Horse	1842-1877	Sioux
Crow Dog	1835?-1910	Brule Sioux
Crowfoot	1821-1890	Blackfoot
Dull Knife	1810-1883	Cheyenne
Gall	1840-1894	Sioux
Geronimo	1829-1909	Apache
Joseph	1840-1904	Nez Perce
Kamiakin	1800?-1909	Apache
Little Crow	1810?-1863	Sioux
Little Turtle	1852-1912	Sioux
Lone Wolf	1820?-1879	Kiowa
Manuelito	1818-1894	Navajo
Massasoit	1580?-1661	Wampanoag
Mato-tope	1800-1837	Mandan
Oconostota	1710?-1785	Cherokee
Opothleyahoolo	1798-1862	Creek
Osceola	1804?-1838	Tallassees
Ouray	1820?-1880	Ute-Apache
Phillip	1639?-1676	Wampanoag
Pontiac	1720-1769	Ottawa
Powhatan	1547?-1618	Powhatan
Quanah Parker	1847-1911	Comanche
Red Cloud	1822-1909	Ogalala Sioux
Red Eagle	1780?-1824	Creek
Roman Nose	1830-1868	Cheyenne
Santanta	1820-1878	Kiowa
Sitting Bull	1831-1890	Sioux
Spotted Tail	1833?-1881	Brule Sioux
Standing Bear	1829?-1908	Ponca
Tall Bull	1815?-1869	Cheyenne
Tecumseh	1768-1813	Shawnee
Victorio	1825?-1880	Apache
Washakie	1804?-1904	Shoshoni

28. Famous Native American Indians

John Louis Clarke	wood sculptor
Charles Curtis	U.S. vice president
Sacajawea	interpretor for Lewis and Clark
Ira Hayes	marine who helped raise flag at Iwo Jima
Hiawatha	founder of Iroquois Confederacy
Pocahontas	legendary lifesaver of Captain John Smith
Will Rogers	humorist
Mitchell Silas	Navajo sand painter
Squanto	interpretor in negotiations between the Pilgrims and Massasoit
Jim Thorpe	Olympic champion, pro football player
Clarence Tinker	U.S. Army General in World War II
Annie Dodge Wauneka	Navajo spokesperson
Sara Winnemucca	Piute translator and peacemaker

29. U.S. Women's Firsts

Name	First U.S. female . . .	Year
Ann Bradstreet	author in America	1640
Ann Franklin	newspaper editor	1762
Mary Kies	granted a patent	1809
Susan G. Bagley	telegrapher	1846
Frances B. Whitcher	humorist	1846
Elizabeth Blackwell	awarded a medical degree	1849
Antoinette B. Blackwell	ordained minister	1853
E. R. Jones	dentist	1855
Mary Surratt	hanged by U.S. government	1865
Mary Edwards Walker	Medal of Honor recipient	1866
Esther Hobart	justice of the peace	1870
Frances E. Willard	college president	1871
Victoria Woodhull	presidential candidate	1872
Helen Magill	Ph.D. awarded to a woman	1877
Susanna Salter	mayor (Argonia, Kansas)	1887
Naggie L. Walker	bank president	1903
Bessica Raiche	solo flight	1910
Alice Wells	policewoman (Los Angeles)	1910
Harriet Quimby	licensed airplane pilot	1911
Annette A. Adams	federal prosecutor	1914
Jeanette Rankin	member of U.S. House of Representatives	1916
Annette Adams	U.S. district attorney	1918
Opha May Johnson	marine	1918
Marie Luhring	automotive engineer	1920
Nellie Taylor Ross	elected governor of a state	1925
Phoebe Omlie	licensed pilot	1927
Jane Addams	Nobel Peace Prize recipient	1931
Amelia Earhart	transatlantic solo flight	1932
Hattie Caraway	elected to U.S. Senate	1932
Frances Perkins	cabinet member (Labor)	1933
Helen Richey	commercial airline pilot	1934
Gretchen Schoenleber	stock exchange member	1935
Georgia N. Clark	Treasurer of the United States	1949
Eugenie M. Anderson	United States ambassador	1949
Jerrie Mock	solo flight around the world	1964
Diane Crump	jockey in Kentucky Derby	1970
Billie Jean King	athlete to earn $100,000 a year	1971
Janet Gray Hayes	mayor of major city (San Jose)	1974
Sandra Day O'Connor	member of U.S. Supreme Court	1981
Dr. Sally K. Ride	astronaut to ride in space	1983
Geraldine A. Ferraro	candidate for vice president	1984
Kathryn D. Sullivan	astronaut to walk in space	1984
Libby Riddles	winner of Iditarod dogsled race	1985
Robin Ahrens	FBI agent killed on duty	1985
Lynette Woodard	member of Harlem Globetrotters	1985
Capt. Linda Bray	to lead American troop in combat	1989

30. Abolitionists

James Gillespie Birney
Antoinette (Brown) Blackwell
John Brown
Olympia Brown
Elizabeth Buffum Chase
William Ellery Channing
Lydia Maria Child
George William Curtis
Fredrick Douglas
William Lloyd Garrison
Robert Ingersoll

Elijah Lovejoy
Samuel Joseph May
Lucretia Mott
Wendell Phillips
Elizabeth Cady Stanton
Lucy Stone
Sojourner Truth
Harriet Tubman
John Woolman
Elizur Wright

31. Confederate States

Alabama
Arkansas
Florida
Georgia
Louisiana
Mississippi
North Carolina
South Carolina
Tennessee
Texas
Virginia

32. Rights Under the Confederate Constitution

While modeled after the United States Constitution, the Constitution of the Conferate States also included the following rights:

- Slavery was legal, although foreign slave trade was banned
- The terms of the President and the Vice-President were six years, and the President was prohibited from serving consecutive terms.
- Congress was not permitted to levy protective tariffs, make appropriations for internal improvements, or to award bounties.
- Cabinet members received non-voting seats in Congress.
- A two-thirds vote of Congress was needed to admit new states.
- The President had the power of the line-item veto in appropriation bills.

33. Advantages of the North

- superior railway system
- 3/4's of the national wealth
- had control of the sea
- industrial capacity
- access to overseas supplies and markets
- twice as many people
- larger army

34. Advantages of the South

- large territory
- well-trained officers
- expert leadership of Robert E. Lee
- fighting for independence
- did not need victory, but only a draw
- defensive strategy

35. Civil War Military Leaders

North
Burnside, Ambrose
Butler, Benjamin F.
Doubleday, Abner
Farragut, David
Foote, Andrew
Fremont, John C.
Grant, Ulysses S.
Halleck, Henry W.
Hancock, Winfield S.
Hooker, Joseph
Logan, John
McClellan, George
Meade, George
Miles, Nelson
Porter, Fitz-John
Rosecrans, William S.
Sheridan, Phillip
Sherman, William T.
Thomas, George
Wallace, Lew
Wilkes, Charles

South
Beauregard, Pierre G. T.
Bragg, Braxton
Breckinridge, John C.
Buckner, Simon Bolivar
Early, Jubal
Ewell, Richard
Forrest, Nathan
Hampton, Wade
Hood, John
Jackson, Stonewall
Johnston, Albert S.
Johnston, Joseph E.
Lee, Robert E.
Longstreet, James
Morgan, John
Mosby, John
Pickett, George
Polk, Leonidas
Semmes, Raphael
Smith, Edmund K.
Stuart, James E. B.
Watie, Stand
Wheeler, Joseph

THE SURRENDER OF LEE TO GRANT AT APPOMATTOX COURT HOUSE

36. Weaponry of the Civil War

Bowie knife
sabre
bayonet
field cannon
garrison cannon
Gatling gun
grenades
land mines
musket
minié rifle
naval mines
naval swivel cannon
pistol
revolving rifle
revolver
rocket
smoothbore guns

37. Civil War Firsts

aerial photograph
aerial reconnaissance
ambulance corps
battle photography
cigarette tax
flame throwers
hospital ships
income tax
ironclad ships
machine gun
military draft
night flares
nursing corps
ready-made clothing factory
repeating rifles
smoke screen
U.S. Navy admiral

38. Songs Popular During the Civil War

Abide With Me
All Quiet on the Potomac
Annie Lisle
Aura Lee
Battle Cry of Freedom
Battle Hymm of the Republic (North)
Beautiful Dreamer
The Bonnie Blue Flag
Choosing a Man Is a Delicate Thing
Dixie (South)
Flag of Columbia
Gobber Peas
Holy! Holy! Holy! Lord God Almighty
John Brown's Body (North)
Johnny Schmoker
Just Before the Battle, Mother
Killarney
Kingdom Coming
La Paloma
Marching Through Georgia (North)
Maryland, My Maryland (South)
Oh Where, Oh Where Has My Little Dog Gone
Old Black Joe
Parade
Shenandoah
Streets of Laredo
Sweet and Low
Tenting on the Old Camp Ground (North)
Tramp, Tramp, Tramp (North)
The Vacant Chair
Weeping Sad and Lonely
When Johnny Comes Marching Home

39. Major Civil War Battles and Campaigns

1861

Fort Sumter	Apr.
Bull Run	July

1862

Ft. Donaldson	Feb.
Monitor and Merrimack	Mar.
Shiloh	April
Fair Oaks	May-June
Seven Days	June-July
Second Bull Run	Aug.
Antietam	Sept.
Perrysville	Oct.
Fredericksburg	Dec.

1863

Murfreesboro	Jan.
Vicksburg	Apr.-July
Chancellorsville	Apr.-May
Gettysburg	July
Chickamauga	Sept.
Chattanooga	Nov.

1864

The Wilderness	May
Spotsylvania Court House	May
Cold Harbor	June
Petersburg	June-July
Mobile Bay blockade	Aug.
Atlanta Campaign	May-Aug.
Sherman's March	Nov.-Dec.
Nashville	Dec.

40. Terms Popularized by the Civil War

antebellum	kit
A.W.O.L.	The Medal of Honor
copperhead	pup tent
doughboy	skedaddle
draftee	Springfields (rifles)
ensign	Tarheel
federal income tax	unconditional surrender
greenbacks	war correspondent
ironclads	

41. Flags Flown over Texas

Spain	Republic of Texas
France	Confederate States
Mexico	United States

42. Important Roads, Trails, and Canals

Appalachian Trail
Boston Post Road
Bozeman Trail
Braddock's Road
California Trail
Champlain Canal
Chesapeake and Delaware Canal
Chisholm Trail
Cumberland Road
El Camino Real
Erie Canal
Lancaster Pike
Mohawk Trail
Mormon Trail
Natchez Trace
National Road
Old Spanish Road
Oregon Trail
Santa Fe Trail
Santee Canal
Wilderness Road

43. Major Events of 1876

Sioux Indians ordered to return to reservations

National League of Professional Baseball formed

Secretary of War, William Belknap, resigns in kickback scandal

Alexander Graham Bell patents the telephone

Centennial Exposition to celebrate 100th anniversary of the Declaration of Independence begins in Philadelphia

Mimeograph invented by Thomas Edison

Gen. George Custer defeated at Little Bighorn

First female admitted to the American Medical Association (S. H. Stevenson)

Colorado admitted at 38th state

First crematory built (in Washington D.C.)

Controversial election of Rutherford B. Hayes over Samuel Tilden

Boss Tweed, convicted of fraud, is caught in Spain and returned to New York City

First American cooking school opened (New York City)

Railroad bridge collapse in Ohio killed 84 *Pacific Express* passengers

Baseball catcher's mask invented

Johns Hopkins University opened in Baltimore

First Ph.D. awarded to a black (by Yale)

American Chemical Society founded

Greenback Party held its first national convention

First tennis court built in the United States (Boston)

189 killed in New York City theatre fire

Dewey Decimal System for libraries initiated

First intercollegiate track meet

First cantilever bridge built (Kentucky River)

First tennis tournament in the U.S. was held

44. American Folk Heroes and Heroines

John Alden
Johnny Appleseed
Clara Barton
Daniel Boone
Jim Bowie
John Brown
Kit Carson
"Buffalo Bill" Cody
Davy Crockett
Amelia Earhart
Wyatt Earp
Mike Fink
Benjamin Franklin
Barbara Fritchie
Nathan Hale

Ira Hayes
"Wild Bill" Hickock
Sam Huston
Casey Jones
John Paul Jones
Charles Lindbergh
Annie Oakley
Sam Patch
Zebulon Pike
Pocahontas
Betsy Ross
Capt. John Smith
Jim Thorpe
Sergeant York

45. Infamous Outlaws of the West

Apache Kid
Sam Bass
William Bonney (Billy the Kid)
Rube Burrow
Dalton brothers (Emmett, Gratton, William & Robert)
Billy Doolin
King Fisher
John Wesley Hardin
Frank James
Jesse James
Henry Plummer
John Reno
Cole Younger

46. States Claiming the Most Presidents

Virginia
George Washington
Thomas Jefferson
James Madison
James Monroe
William Henry Harrison
John Tyler
Zachary Tyler
Woodrow Wilson

Ohio
Ulysses S. Grant
Rutherford B. Hayes
James A. Garfield
Benjamin Harrison
William McKinley
William Howard Taft
Warren G. Harding

47. Sailing Vessels

bark
barkentine
brig
brigantine
catamaran
clipper
cutter
frigate
galleon
junk
ketch
merchantman
schooner
sloop
wherry
yawl

48. Slang of the 1890's

© 1992 by Prentice-Hall

Slang	Meaning	Slang	Meaning
ankle	walk	plug	a silver dollar
bindle	blanket roll	plunk	a dollar
cheek	boldness	plute	rich person
chew the fat	to talk	rat	an informer, spy
chin	to talk	sand	bravery, courage
close shave	narrow escape	shake a leg	hurry
crush	infatuation	shantytown	poor neighborhood
daily bread	household wage earner	shove off	leave
doggy	well groomed	simoleon	a dollar
dough	money	slam	a cutting comment
fink	scab, strikebreaker	small-bore	unimportant
foot-slogger	foot soldier	smooth	very good
geezer	man, guy	snap, a	easy
glad rags	best clothes	sneakers	athletic shoes
good-looker	attractive person	spinach	a beard
grandstand	to show off	steady	boy/girl friend
gunboats	shoes	step out	go to a party
gun moll	female criminal	stone broke	without any money
hardtack	money	stuck on	in love with
hoity-toity	snobbish, uppity	swivet	heated rage
hornswoggle	to cheat	tacky	in poor taste
hot	fast, speedy	tad	a young boy
jim-dandy	good, satisfactory	take the cake	win
jitney	a nickel	tightwad	miserly person
loco	crazy	well-heeled	wealthy
long green	money	willies, the	very anxious
mitt	hand		
piffle	nonsense!		
pipe down	be quiet!		

49. Fads and Fancies of the 1890's

And Her Name Was Maud comic strip
bicycling
cakewalk (dance)
chewing gum
comic pictures
commemorative spoons
croquet
floral parades for automobiles
Foxy Grandpa comic strips
hootchy kootchy tie
huge hats for women
Gibson girl

lavendar gloves for men
magic latern shows
minstrels
ouija board
petticoats
Pigs-in-Clover puzzles
roller skates
skirt dance
stereoptician
Sunday funnies
trade cards
vaudeville

50. Inventions of Thomas Edison

vote recorder
phonograph
electric incandescent light
motion-picture machine
peep show
talking picture machine
storage battery
cement mixer
dictaphone
duplicating machine
electric lighting plant
electric company

51. Famous Performers of the Nineteenth Centruy

Maurice Barrymore
John Wilkes Booth
Junius Booth
Edwin Booth
William "Buffalo Bill" Cody
Lotta Crabtree
Charlotte Cushman
Louisa Lane Drew
Robert G. Ingersoll
Scott Joplin
Jumbo the Elephant
Jenny Lind
Annie Oakley
John Philip Sousa
Sitting Bull
Gen. Tom Thumb

52. Popular Songs of 1900

A Bird in A Gilded Cage
Because
The Bridge of Sighs
Creole Belle
De Cake Walk Queen
Down By the Riverside
Give Me the Good Old Fashioned Girl
I Can't Tell You Why I Love You, But I Do
I'd Still Believe You True
It's Just Because I Love You So
Jimmy, the Pride of Newspaper Row
Just One Kiss
Lift Every Voice and Sing
Lucinda, I Am Waiting for You
Ma Tiger Lily
Mandy Lee
Midnight Fire Alarm
My Automobile Girl
Nobody Sees Us but the Man in the Moon
Tell Me, Pretty Maiden
The Voodoo Man
When Chloe Sings a Song
When I Think of You
When the Harvest Days Are Over, Jennie Dear
When You Were Sweet Sixteen
You Can't Keep a Good Man Down

53. Prices in 1900

baseball bat 35¢
bathtub $7.25
bicycle $10.50
box camera $3.50
brass bed $3.00
corn 43¢ a bushel
dozen eggs 12¢
Edison phonograph $19.00
eggs 10¢
electric light bulb 30¢
guitar $3.00
ice box $7.00
kerosene lantern 65¢
ladies' hose 15¢ pr.
men's neckties 18¢
men's tailor-made suit $9.00

mixed nuts 15¢ lb.
open buggy $26.00
roll top desk $18.50
safety pins 2¢ doz.
set of false teeth $5.00
sewing machine $12.60
shave and a haircut 25¢ (2 bits)
shirt 23¢
silk 50¢ yd.
Smith & Wesson revolver $10.75
stereoscope 25¢
tin can 10¢
trombone $15.00
turkey dinner 20¢
white dress shirt 60¢
work shirts 18¢

54. Turn of the Century Patent Medicines

Ayer's Cherry Pectoral
Carbonium Rheumatism Cure
Castoria
Chichester's Pennyroyal Pill
Dr. Bell's Pine-Tar-Honey
Dr. Hammond's Nerve and Brain Pills
Dr. M. Bain's Blood Pills
Dr. Rose's Obesity Powder
Electric Liniment
German Liquor Cure
Kid-ne-oids
Lydia E. Pinkham's Vegetable Compound
Mexican Headache Neuralgia and Cure
Mother's Friend
Nectarine
Nervita Pills
Peruna
Sapolio
St. Jacob's Oil
Tonsiline Throat Medicene
Wonderful Little Liver Pills

55. Nineteenth-Century American Authors

Henry Adams
Jane Addams
Louisa May Alcott
Horatio Alger
Gertrude Atherton
George Bancroft
Ambrose Bierce
Ann Bradstreet
William Cullen Bryant
Kate Chopin
James Fenimore Cooper
Stephen Crane
Margaret Deland
Emily Dickinson
Ralph Waldo Emerson
Mary Wilkins Freeman
Margaret Fuller
Horace Greeley
Harlan F. Halsey
Joel Chandler Harris
Bret Harte
Nathaniel Hawthorne
Oliver Wendell Holmes
William Dean Howells
Washington Irving
Henry James

Sidney Lanier
James Russell Lowell
Herman Melville
Clement C. Moore
Petroleum V. Nasby
Edgar Allan Poe
William Sidney Porter (O. Henry)
James Whitcomb Riley
George Ripley
Harriet Beecher Stowe
Booth Tarkington
Henry David Thoreau
Mark Twain
Lewis Wallace
Artemus Ward
Noah Webster
Walt Whitman
John Greenleaf Whittier

56. The Muckrakers

Writer	Areas of Influence
Ray Stannard Baker	labor abuses, unions
William Hard	child labor
Thomas Lawson	stock market manipulation
Charles Edward Russell	tenement living conditions
Upton Sinclair	food processing perils
Lincoln Steffens	corrupt city government
Ida Tarbell	abuses of big business
George Kibbe Turner	corruption and vice

57. Women's Rights Pioneers

Susan B. Anthony
Alice Blackwell
Harriot Blatch
Amelia Bloomer
Lucy Burns
Carrie Chapman Catt
Paula Wright Davis
Crystal Eastman
Isabella Beecher Hooker
Esther Morris
Lucretia Mott
Emmeline Pankhurst
Alice Paul
Anne Smith Peck
Lucy Stone
Elizabeth Cady Stanton
Victoria Woodhull

58. Automobile Brands of 1906

Auburn
Autocar
Berkshire
Buick
Cadillac
Cannon
Columbia
Compound
Corbin
Crawford
Dolson
Duquesne
Duryea
Elmore
Ford
Franklin
Gale
Glide
Jackson
Knox
Lambert
Logan

Marion
Maxwell
Michigan
Mitchell
Moline
Monarch
Northern
Oldsmobile
Orient
Oxford
Pierce
Premier
Queen
Rambler
Reo
St. Louis
Stanhope
Stoddard-Dayton
Walker
Wayne
Wolverine
York
Zent

59. Labor Leaders

Henry Bridges
Cesar Chavez
Eugene Debs
Elizabeth Flynn
Samuel Gompers
Jimmy Hoffa
Mary "Mother" Jones
John L. Lewis
Charles Litchman

George Meany
Frances Perkins
Terrence Powderly
A. Phillip Randolph
Rose Schneiderman
Albert Shanker
Uriah Stephens
William H. Sylvis
William S. Townsend

60. Entrepreneurs Who Shaped American History

Elizabeth Arden	cosmetics
Phillip Armour	meat packing
John Jacob Astor	furs and real estate
P. T. Barnum	entertainment
Alexander G. Bell	telephones
Clarence Birdseye	frozen foods
Asa Candler	soft drinks
Andrew Carnegie	steel
William Colgate	soap, toothpaste
Samuel Colt	guns
Peter Cooper	railroads
Ezra Corwell	telegraph
Robert de Graff	pocket paperbacks
Cecil B. De Mille	movies
John Deere	plows
Eleuthére Irénée Du Pont	gunpowder
William C. Durant	automobiles
George Eastman	photographic equipment
Thomas Edison	electrical equipment, phonograph
Harvey Firestone	tires
Henry Ford	automobiles
J. Paul Getty	oil
Fred Harvey	fast food
H. J. Heinz	food
Howard Hughes	movies, aviation
Henry J. Kaiser	shipbuilding
Will Kellogg	breakfast cereal
Joseph P. Kennedy	banking, entertainment, real estate
Ray Kroc	fast food, McDonalds
Donald McKay	shipbuilding
Sarah McWilliams	cosmetics
J. Pierpont Morgan	banking, steel
Ransom E. Olds	automobiles
Elisha Otis	elevators
John D. Rockefeller	oil
David Sarnoff	broadcasting
R.W. Sears & A.C. Roebuck	mail order sales
Samuel Slater	textiles
Leland Stanford	railroads
Levi Strauss	denim pants
Cornelius Vanderbilt	steamboats, railroads
Charles Walgreen	drugstores
John Wanamaker	department stores
A. Montgomery Ward	mail order sales
Eli Whitney	cotton gin, guns, clocks
Frank W. Woolworth	department stores
William Wrigley, Jr.	chewing gum

© 1992 by Prentice-Hall

61. Terms Contributed by World War I

A.E.F.	dog fight	overseas
Allies	dog tag	red tape
basket case	doughboys	rookie
Big Bertha (gun)	draft dodger	sabotage
blimp	dud	shell shock
buck private	entente	slacker
buddy	flame thrower	sound off
chemical warfare	goldbrick	strafe
chief of staff	hand grenade	tank
chow	hitch	trench warfare
civvies	khaki	U-boat
C.O.	king pin	
convoy	KP	

62. World War I Campaigns Involving the U.S.

1917

Cambrai	Nov.-Dec.

1918

Somme	Mar.-July
Lys	April
Aisne	May-June
Noyon-Montdidier	June
Champagne-Marne	July
Aisne-Marne	July
Somme	Aug.
Oise-Aisne	Aug.-Nov.
Ypres-Lys	Aug.-Nov.
Saint-Mihiel	Sept.
Meuse-Argonne	Sept.-Nov.
Vitorio-Vento	Oct.-Nov.

63. Woodrow Wilson's Fourteen Points

1. Open covenants of peace, openly arrived at.
2. Freedom of navigation on the seas.
3. Removal of economic barriers and equality of trade conditions.
4. Guaranteed reduction in armaments.
5. Impartial adjustment of colonial claims.
6. Evacuation of occupied Russian territories and fair treatment of Russia.
7. Evacuation and restoration of Belgium.
8. Evacuation and restoration of all French territory.
9. Readjustment of Italy's border.
10. Guarantee autonomous development for Austria-Hungary.
11. Restoration of territories of Rumania, Serbia and Montenegro.
12. Assure sovereignty to Turkish portions of Ottoman Empire and assure autonomy to other nationalities under Turkish rule. Free passage through Straits of Dardanelles.
13. Establish an independent Poland.
14. Formation of an association of nations to guarantee political independence and territorial integrity of all nations.

64. Slang of the 1920's

Slang	Meaning	Slang	Meaning
all my whiskers	nonsense!	hoof	to dance
all wet	wrong, incorrect	horsefeathers	nonsense!
and how!	definitely!	hotsie-totsie	very good
audies	sound movies	hyper	excited, thrilled
banana oil	nonsense	jalopy	an old car
barnstorm	tour the country doing aurplane shows	Jane	a plain girl
		jinny	a speakeasy
bathtub gin	homemade gin	juice-joint	a speakeasy
bee's knees	great!	keen	attractive, good
berries, the	the best	kisser	the mouth
between a rock and a hard place	in a difficult situation	lickety-split	quickly
		lousy	bad, inferior
big cheese	an important person	lug	a dull man
bim	girl friend	main drag	main street
blind dragon	chaperone	malarkey	lies, nonsense
blind pig	a speakeasy	nitwit	idiot
blotto	drunk	nuts	nonsense!
bootleg	make or sell illegal liquor	park	made out in a car
breeze in	drop in unexpectedly	pash	passion
bug wash	hair oil	pip-squeak	a useless person
bull session	group discussion	rah-rah	overly enthusiastic
bunk	nonsense!	raspberries	nonsense!
caper	a robbery	ricky tick	ragtime music of 20's
carhop	waitress at a drive-in restaurant	ritzy	elegant
		rock	a dollar
cat's, the	outstanding	sad sack	an odd person
cat's meow	outstanding	sheba	girl friend
cat's pajamas	good, super	sheik	handsome man
cheaters	eyeglasses	sloppy	messy
chopper	submachine gun	smooch	kiss/hug
crush	being infatuated with	speakie	a movie with sound
darb	excellent	struggle buggy	car
dig dirt	to gossip	stuffy	prudish
divine	nice, enjoyable	swell	fine
do in	to eat a ——-	talkie	movie with sound
fat cat	wealthy person	tin Lizzie	Model T Ford
flapper	uninhibited woman, a style of dressing	white cow	vanilla milkshake
		wise up	become aware, learn
flick	movie	wish book	catalog
fridge	refrigerator	wowser	prude, self-righteous person
gaga	crazy, silly		
get hot!	Dance! Go for it!		
giggle-water	whiskey, liquor		
goon	a thug, ruffian		
governor	father, one's superior		
grand	good		
ham-and-egger	ordinary person		
high hat	to snub someone		

65. Fads and Fancies of the 1920's

art deco
auto camping
baggy knickers
bathtub gin
bobbed hair for women
Burma Shave road signs
center-parted,
 patent-leather hair
the Charleston
cloche hats
crossword puzzles
dance marathons
flagpole sitting
flappers
Florida land boom
hip flasks

jazz
King Tut hats
Mah Jong
mascara
neon lights
Oxford bag (pants)
pajamas as daily wear
peekaboo hats
raccoon coats
radio
silent movies
speakeasies
Stutz Bearcat
tams
turned down hose

66. The Alphabet of the New Deal

AAA	Agricultural Adjustment Act
CCC	Civilian Conservation Corps
FERA	Federal Emergency Relief Act
FHA	Federal Housing Administration
HOLC	Home Owners' Loan Corporation
NRA	National Recovery Administration
NYA	National Youth Administration
PWA	Public Works Administration
REA	Rural Electrification Administration
SEC	Securities and Exchange Commission
TVA	Tennessee Valley Authority
USHA	United States Housing Authority
WPA	Works Progress Administration

67. Slang of the 1930's

Slang	Meaning	Slang	Meaning
alligator	a fan of jive/swing music	one and only	sweetheart
		phooey	nonsense!
back burner	to postpone	sad sack	unpopular student
body and soul	girl/boy friend	screwball	an odd person
boog	to dance	scuttlebutt	rumor
boondoogle	project wasting public funds	session	a party
		Shangri La	paradise
buttinski	nosey person	smart Alec	wise guy
cannon fodder	regular soldier	smoke eater	a firefighter
crabber	nagging critic	snooty	snobbish
creep	obnoxious person	spinach	nonsesne!
cut a rug	dance	threads	clothing
dinger	telephone	tops	the best
dizzy	odd, strange	twerp	disgusting
doodle-bug	jalopy, buggy	unlax	relax
doozy	wonderful person or thing	up the wall	crazy
		wacko!	great!
Dust Bowl	Great Plains states	whodunit	detective story
G-man	FBI agent	with bells on	definitely
grease	a bribe	woof	to chat
have kittens	to get excited	zombie	weird person
high hat	arrogant, superior	zoo suit	special type of man's suit
Hoover blanket	newspaper used as blanket by homeless		
jam session	musicians playing as a group		
jerk	a fool, disliked person		
lovebirds	sweethearts		
Nervous Nellie	anxious person		

68. Fads and Fancies of the 30's

Betty Boop
big apple (dance)
bingo
boogie (dance)
broomstick dresses
Buck Rogers Disintegrator Ray guns
candid camera photography
contract bridge
Eugenie hat
fox trot (dance)
handies (game)
jigsaw puzzles
jitterbug
Lindy hop (dance)
Lambeth walk (dance)
memory games
Mickey Mouse
miniature golf
Monopoly®
pickle (dance)
roller skating
rumba (dance)
saddle shoes
shag (dance)
Shorty George (dance)
skiing
softball
swing
tent dress
two piece swim suits (women)
zoot suits

69. American Automobiles of the 30's

Auburn
American Austin
American Bantum
Buick
Cadillac
Chevrolet
Chrysler
Cord
DeSoto
Doble
Dodge
Duesenberg
Erksine
Essex
Ford
Franklin
Graham
Hudson
Hupmobile
LaFayette

LaSalle
Lincoln
Marmon
Marquette
Nash
Oakland
Oldsmobile
Packard
Pierce-Arrow
Plymouth
Pontiac
Reo
Rockne
Roosevelt
Studebaker
Stutz
Terraplane
Viking
Whippet
Willys

70. Major Films of 1939

Cat and the Canary, The
Dark Vickory
Destiny Rides Again
Drums Along the Mohawk
Gone With the Wind
Goodybe, Mr. Chips
Gunga Din
Mr. Smith Goes to Washington
Roaring Twenties, The
Stage Coach
Ugly Duckling, The
Wizard of Oz, The
Women, The
Wuthering Heights

71. Slang of the 1940's

Slang	Meaning
ameche	to telephone
b.y.t	bright young things
bag	to shoot down a plane
barouche	car, jalopy
brainchild	someone's creative idea
bunny	to chat
city slicker	dandy from the city
corny	unimportant, passe
cosy	comfortable
creep	despicable person
eager beaver	enthusiastic helper
fuddy-duddy	old-fashioned person
gobbledygook	double talk, long speech
gone with the wind	run off (with the money)
grandstand	to show off
grotty	new but useless
hi-de-ho	hello
in cahoots with	conspiring with
lettuce	money
old hat	out-dated
pass the buck	pass responsibility for
pennies from heaven	easy money

72. Fads and Fancies of the 1940's

bebop
bubble gum blowing contests
fast gun clubs
flying saucers
jitterbug
"new look" women's fashion
pinafore dresses
Rosie the Riveter
slinky
tutti-frutti
victory gardens
zoot suit

73. Popular Radio Shows of the 1940's

The Abbott and Costello Show
The Adventures of Bulldog Drummond
The Adventures of Father Brown
The Adventures of Topper
Amos and Andy Show
Arthur Godfrey's Talent Scouts
Beulah
The Bickersons
Bing Crosby Show
Blackstone the Magic Detective
Calamity Jane
Captain Midnight
The Carters of Elm Street
Challenge of the Yukon
The Cisco Kid
Colonel Stoopnagle and Budd
Death Valley Days
The Dinah Shore Show
Dr. IQ
Duffy's Tavern
Edgar Bergen and
    Charlie McCarthy Show
Fibber McGee and Molly
Gene Autrey's Melody Ranch
The George Burns and
    Gracie Allen Show
The Grand Ole Opry
The Great Gildersleeve
The Green Hornet
Inner Sanctum Mysteries
It Pays to Be Ignorant
The Jack Benny Program
Leave It to the Girls
The Life of Riley

The Lone Ranger
Ma Perkins
Major Hoople
Maudie's Diary
The Mercury Wonder Show
Mrs. Miniver
Nick Carter, Master Detective
Our Miss Brooks
Perry Mason
Queen for a Day
Red Ryder
The Red Skelton Show
The Roy Rogers Show
The Saturday Morning Vaudeville
    Theatre
Scattergood Baines
Sherlock Holmes
Sky King
Stage Door Canteen
Stella Dallas
The Thin Man
20 Questions
Uncle Walter's Dog House
What's the Name of That
    Tune?
The Whistler
You Bet Your Life
Young Dr. Malone
Your Hit Parade

74. Terms Contributed by World War II

amphibious landing
atomic bomb
Axis
bazooka
black market
blitz
blitzkrieg
boondocks
commando
concentration camp
cover for
D-Day
Dear John letter
draft dodger
ersatz
fascist
five star general
flak
GI Joe

gizmo
gobbledygook
gremlin
gung ho
home front
Jeep
Johnny-come-lately
kamikaze
Lend Lease
Liberty ship
Nazi
ninety-day wonder
nylon
Panzers
PFC
pinup
POW
propaganda
PT boat

PX
Quonset hut
radar
R and R
rationing
Rosie the Riveter
saturation bombing
scorched earth policy
snorkel
storm troopers
USO
V.D.
WAACS
WAVES
WAFS
walkie talkie
war bonds
war brides

75. Five Star Generals

Omar N. Bradley
Dwight D. Eisenhower
Douglas MacArthur
George C. Marshall
Henry "Hap" Arnold

76. Items Rationed During World War II

butter
canned foods
cheese
coffee
fats

gasoline
meats
oils
shoes
sugar

77. Slang of the 1950's

Slang	Meaning	Slang	Meaning
a gas	great; super	hoo-boy	Oh, boy!
a groove	superb	hood	small-time criminal
beat	tired	hot dog	a show-off
beatnik	person indifferent to society	howdy doody	hello
birdie biker	female motorcyclist	idiot box	televison
blast	a good time	iggle	to persuade
blast off	scram	in the groove	enjoying jazz
boo	excellent	jumbo size	large, huge
bread hooks	hands	kicks	thrills; fun
buddy buddy	very friendly	lose your cool	get angry
buddy seat	motorcycle sidecar	make the scene	arrive; attend
bug	bother	nerf-bar	car's bumper
bug out	to leave	nowhere	not hep; square
burp gun	sub-machine gun	off the wall	strange
chiller-diller	a very scary movie	out of sight	great, unbelievable
chintzy	cheap, low quality	passion pit	drive-in theatre
clutz	awkward person, nerd	pad	home
cool	superb; acceptable	payola	money
cowabunga	hello	rip off	take advantage of
cut out	to leave	rumble	fight; brawl
daddy-o	man, dad	scaggy	disgusting
dead head	dunce, a bore	sends me	excites me
deb's delight	eligible bachelor	shag	to leave
deepie	3-D movie	shim	one who dislikes rock and roll music
deke	to renege, back out		
dicey	risky	shook up	excited, alarmed
dig	understand, appreciate	shrink	psychiatrist
dingaling	odd person, nerd	sick	deranged, mentally ill
disc jockey	radio show host	skins	tires
disco	a discoteque	slay	to impress
do your own thing	express yourself	sock hop	a dance
		space cadet	a strange person
downer	an unpleasant experience	spaced out	high on drugs
drag	anyone or anything dull or boring	split	to leave
		square	old fashioned person
dream-boat	an attractive male	teenager	person 13-19 years old
dullsville	boring	the end	tops; the very best
far out	outstanding	tired blood	without energy
flip	get very excited	turf	territory
flaked out	exhausted; tired	twist	a kind of dance
funny money	counterfeit bills	vibes	aura a person projects
get it together	straighten out one's life	way out	excellent
get-up-and-go	energy, pep	whirly-bird	helicopter
glitch	obstacle	wig out	go crazy
goof	to make a mistake	with it	in style, hep
greaser	person with long oily hair	yoyo	nerd
hardeeharhar	false laughter at a bad joke	yuck!	expression of disgust
hairy	difficult	zorch	super
hep or hip	enlightened		

78. Fads and Fancies of the 1950's

ankle bracelets
apaches (male's haircuts)
automobile stuffing
beatniks
Bermuda shorts
black leather jackets
black stockings
blue suede shoes
bomb shelters
bop (dance)
bowling
bunny hop (dance)
bucket purses
calypso (dance)
car stuffing
chemise dresses
circle, the (dance)
come-as-you-are parties
coonskin caps
crew cut
crinolines
cufflinks, huge
doe eyes
droodles
ducktails (haircuts)
false eyelashes
felt skirts with appliqued
 poodles
fender skirts for cars
flat tops (haircuts)
flower power
garrison belts
hand jive (dance)
horse operas (westerns)
Hollywood exhaust pipes
Howdy-Doody
hula-hoops
Indian moccasins
juke box
jumbo size large, huge
jungle jackets
knock-knock jokes
long sideburns

mowhawks (males' haircuts)
moon hub caps
motorcycle jackets
Mouseketeers
paste-on rhinestones
paint-by-number kits
panty raids
pegged pants
phone booth stuffing
picture windows
pizza
pompadour hair cut
pony tails
poodle cut
pop beads
"post office"
propeller topped beannies
sack dresses
saddle shoes
Scrabble®
shirttails out
short shorts
silly putty
sideburns
slinkies
slop, the (dance)
soap operas
sock hops
"spin the bottle"
suburbia
sword pins
tail fins on cars
3-D movies
waxed hair
white bucks (shoes)
white lipstick
white socks
white sportcoats

79. Rock Stars of the 1950's

Paul Anka
Frankie Avalon
Chuck Berry
Big Bopper
Pat Boone
Freddy Cannon
Chubby Checker
Dee Clark
Eddie Cochran
Floyd Cramer
Bobby Darin
Jimmy Dean
Bo Diddley
Duane Eddy
Everly Brothers
Fabian (Forte)
Fats Domino
Connie Francis

Bobie Freeman
Bill Haley
Buddy Holly
Tab Hunter
Jerry Lee Lewis
Little Anthony
Little Richard
Sal Mineo
Ricky Nelson
Sandy Nelson
Roy Orbison
Carl Perkins
Elvis Presley
Lloyd Price
Marty Robbins
Jimmie Rodgers
Bobby Rydell
Tommy Sands
Jack Scott

Neil Sedaka
Dotie Stevens
Johnny Tillotson
Conway Twitty
Richie Valens
Bobby Vee
Gene Vincent

80. Rock Groups of the 1950's

The Blue Notes
The Browns
The Champs
The Chantels
The Cleftones
The Coasters
The Crescendos
The Crests
The Crew Cuts
The Crickets
Danny & the Juniors
The Dells
The Diamonds
Dion & the Belmonts
The Del Vikings
Dickey Doo & the Don'ts
Dion & the Belmonts
Drifters

The Dubs
The Fireballs
The Five Satins
The Flamingos
The Fleetwoods
The Four Coins
The Four Freshmen
The Four Lads
The Four Preps
Frankie Lymon & the Teenagers
The Heartaches
The Isley Brothers
Jan & Dean
The Jesters
Joe Bennett & the Sparktones
Johnny & the Hurricanes
Little Richard and the Imperials
The Miracles

The Moonglows
The Platters
The Playmates
The Shirelles
The Skyliners
The Turbans

81. Hit Television Shows of the 1950's

Gunsmoke
Walt Disney
Red Skelton
I Love Lucy
Dragnet
You Bet Your Life
The Jack Benny Show
Ed Sullivan Show
Danny Thomas Show
Wagon Train
I've Got a Secret
General Electric Theatre
The Jackie Gleason Show
Colgate Comedy Hour
Candid Camera
Lassie
Have Gun Will Travel
December Bride
Perry Mason
Perry Como Show
The Millionaire
$64,000 Question
The Real McCoys
Mama
What's My Line?
Lawrence Welk Show
Ford Theatre

82. Slang of the 1960's

Slang	Meaning	Slang	Meaning
ankle biters	little children	glitch	an obstacle
bad scene	an unpleasant event	go ape	lose control
bat phone	police officer's phone	go-go	of discotheques or a style of music
beach buggy	open vehicle drive on the sand	go with the flow	to relax, be passive
beach bunny	non-surfing girl at the beach	greaser	person with long oily hair
birdie biker	female motorcyclist		
boss	super	groddy	disgusting
boxes	guitars	gross	repulsive
brain drain	emigration of a country's scientists	grossed out	disgusted
		groovy	outstanding
bum trip	an unpleasant event	hack	cope
bummer	unpleasant experience	hang a left	make a left turn
bug	to annoy someone	hang loose	relax
bummer	a bad experience	hang-up	problem
catch some rays	sunbathe	happening	special event
chick	a young woman	hawk	war supporter
clanked	tired	heavy	powerful
clutz	awkward person	hood	small-time, petty criminal
cool it	calm down		
copping out	renege; break a promise	hot dog	show-off
crash pad	place to sleep	hustle	to persuade or pressure
deb's delight	eligible bachelor	mod	modern; in fashion
dingaling	an odd person; nerd	mop-top	one with a Beatle haircut
do your own thing	do it your way		
		mover	influential person
dove	peace lover	nifty	useful; good
downer	an unpleasant experience	No way!	Definitely not!
dropout	nonconformist	now	fashionable
dullsville	boring	off the wall	strange
fab	attractive; exciting	out of sight	great; unbelievable
far out	great; outstanding	pad	bed, place to sleep
fink out	to back out, quit	payola	money; a bribe
flake off	scram	pits	disgusting; unpleasant
flower child	hippie, member of the counterculture	plastic	artificial, fake
		psychedelic	bright, dreamy patterns of light or color
for real	truly; indeed		
freedom riders	civil rights protestors	rag top	convertible
funny money	counterfeit bills	rap	to talk, chart
funky	excellent	rap session	discussion
gasser	the very best	rat fink	detestable person
generation gap	difference between youth and their parents	right on	yes, okay
		rip off	robbery, theft
get it together	straighten out one's life	shades	sunglasses
get-up-and-go	energy; pep	shot down	rejected

82. Slang of the 1960's, continued

Slang	Meaning	Slang	Meaning
shrink	psychiatrist	tough toenails	too bad
shuck	a phony	trash	to destroy
sit in	to take over an area in protest	tuff	excellent
		tune in	pay attention
spaced out	high on drugs	tune out	ignore
spiffy	neat; good	turn off	to repulse someone
squaresville	a dull place	uncool	bad; tense
straight	not using drugs	unreal	outstanding
street people	the homeless or poor	uptight	nervous, tense
sweat	to worry	vibes	person's aura
teenie bopper	young teen rock fan	whiz kid	intelligent child
tell it like it is	talk candidly	wow	fantastic!
		yuck!	expression of disgust
the man	anyone in authority	zap	wipe out; defeat
threads	clothes	zilch	zero
together	free of anxiety	zit	pimple
total	completely demolish	zot	zero

83. Fads and Fancies of the 60's

acid rock
Alligator, The (dance)
Arab kaftans
astrology
Barbie® dolls
bare feet
Batman merchandise
beehive hairdos
beards
The Beatles
bell bottom pants
Batman
body painting
bouffant hair-do
circle pins
communes
computer dating
cosmic consciousness
dune buggy
Eskino muk luks
flowers on jeans
frisbee
Frug (dance)
Funky Chicken (dance)
Haight Ashbury
hair ironing
hippie costumes
incense

go-go dancing
granny glasses
harmonicas
hootenannies
huge sunglasses
Hully-Gully (dance)
"instant insanity" puzzles
ironing hair
Jerk, The (dance)
leather pants
light shows
love beads
love chains
Mickey Mouse watches
mini-skirts
mop-top haircut (males)
Monkey (dance)
multicolor painted vans
navy pea coats
Nehru collars
new math
paisley clothing
panty hose
paper clothes
piano wrecking
pigtails on men
pillbox hat

pop art
Princeton haircut (males)
protest buttons
psychedelic posters
rocking chairs
skateboarding
spike heels
Superball®
surfer styles
surfing
T p'ing (toilet papering)
tarot fortune-telling cards
teased hair
thigh high boots
toe rings
trampolines
transcendental meditation
trivia contests
The Twist
underground newspapers
unisex clothing
very long hair
Volkswagon beetles
Watusi (dance)
wet-look fabrics
Woodies (station wagons)
worry beads

84. Hit Records of 1960

Alley Oop
Are You Lonesome Tonight?
Cathy's Clown

El Paso
Exodus
Everybody's Somebody's Fool
I'm Sorry
It's Now or Never
Itsy Bitsy Bikini
I Want to Be Wanted
Mister Custer
My Heart Has a Mind of Its Own
Running Bear
Save the Last Dance for Me
Sink the Bismark
The Sound of Music
Stay
Stuck on You
Teen Angel
Theme From a Summer Place
Why

85. Bestselling Fiction of 1968

Airport   Hailey
Couples   Updike
The First Circle   Solzhenitsyn
The Hurricane Years   Hawley
Preserve and Protect   Drury
The Queen's Confession   Holt
Red Sky in the Morning   Bradford
The Senator   Pearson
Tell Me How Long the Trains Been Gone   Baldwin
Testimony of Two Men   Caldwell
The Tower of Babel   West
The Triumph   Galbraith
True Grit   Portis
Tunc   Durrell
Vanished   Knebel
A World of Profit   Auclincloss

86. Major Events of 1968

Southern California defeated Indiana 14-3 in the Rose Bowl.
Synthetic DNA was first produced.
USS Pueblo seized by the North Koreans.
Tet offensive was initiated in South Vietnam.
Super Bowl II was won by the Green Bay Packers.
Martin Luther King, Jr. was assassinated.
Riots broke out in 125 cities.
Nixon and Humphrey were nominated for president.
Poor People's March held in Washington, D.C.
Peace talks with North Vietnam began in Paris.
Robert Kennedy was assassinated.
Nuclear nonproliferation treaty was signed.
U.S. Open tennis championship was won by Arthur Ashe.
Democratic National Convention resulted in violent clash between anti-war
   protestors and Chicago police.
Bombing of North Vietnam began.
Helen Keller, John Steinbeck, Upton Sinclair, and Edna Ferber died.
Students struck at San Francisco State College.
The first woman was added to the FBI's most wanted list.
Films, *2001 Space Odyssey, Rosemary's Baby,* and *Yellow Submarine* were released.
Olympic games were held in Mexico City.
Peggy Fleming won the Olympic gold medal for figure skating.
Oliver! won the Academy Award for best picture.
Jackie Kennedy married Aristotle Onasis.
Richard Nixon was elected President.
First American astronauts oribited the earth.
First NFL-AFL football draft was held.
Pete Maravich's 44.2 points per game won the NCAA Division I basketball
   scoring title.
Freeze dried coffee was introduced.
Shirley Chisholm, first black female U.S. Representative, was elected.
Simon and Garfunkel won a Grammy Award for *Mrs. Robinson.*
First U.S. heart transplant performed by Dr. Denton Cooley.
Southern California's O. J. Simpson won the Heisman Trophy.

87. Automobile Firsts

steam truck	1769
four-wheel drive vehicle	1824
2-stroke gas engine	1860
gas-powered motor car	1875
4-stroke gas engine	1877
pneumatic car tire	1885
electric car	1887
U.S. automobile company (Duryea)	1894
automobile race	1895
magnito ignition	1897
auto license plate (NY)	1901
AAA founded	1905
supercharged engine	1907
Model-T Ford introduced	1907
drive-in gas station	1913
water-cooled V-8 engine	1914
car radio (Marconiphone)	1922
motel (San Luis Obispo)	1924
drive-in theater	1933
parking meters (Oklahoma City)	1935
pop-up headlights (Cord)	1936
air-conditioned auto (Packard)	1939
superhighway (Pennsylvania)	1940
tubeless tires	1948
tinted windows	1950
front-wheel disk brakes (Citroën)	1955
drive-in restaurant (McDonalds)	1955
solar-powered car	1955
air bag safety cushion (GM)	1973

88. Terms Contributed by the Vietnam War

defoliate
DMZ
domino theory
fire fight
Green Berets
grunt
Ho Chi Minh trail
MIA

napalm
protective reaction
Viet Cong
dove
Silent Majority
teach-in
peacenik
Yippies

89. Wars Involving the United States

Revolutionary War
War of 1812
Mexican War
Civil War
Spanish-American War
World War I
World War II
Korean War
Vietnam War
Persian Gulf War

90. Significant Ships in American History

Alabama
Arizona
Bon Homme Richard
Clermont
Constitution (Old Ironsides)
Cutty Sark
Essex
Intrepid
Lawrence
Luisitania

Maine
Mayflower
Merrimac
Monitor
Nautilus
Niagara
Oklahoma
PT 109
Pueblo
Savannah
United States

91. Treaties Signed by the U.S.

Treaty	Date	Main Provisions
Treaty of Paris	1783	U.S. and Great Britain following Revolutionary War. American independence recognized.
Jay Treaty	1794-1795	U.S. and Britain each agreed to arbitrate financial claims of their citizens.
Pinckney Treaty	1795	Spain recognized the Mississippi as the western boundary of the U.S.
Louisiana Purchase	1803	France sold territory to U.S., doubling U.S. area.
Treaty of Ghent	1814	U.S. and Great Britain following War of 1812. Reestablished pre-war boundaries of the U.S.
Rush-Bagot Treaty	1817	Limited U.S. and British armaments on Great Lakes
Adams-Onis Treaty	1819	Spain agreed on sale of Florida and the boundary between Mexico and Oregon country.
Webster-Ashburton Treaty	1842	U.S. and Great Britain settled boundary dispute over Maine.
Guadalupe Hildago	1848	Treaty following Mexican War by which Mexico recognized Rio Grande as border of Texas and gave up claim to California and New Mexico.
Treaty of Paris	1898	Treaty with Spain following Spanish-American War in which Puerto Rico was ceded to U.S. and Philippine Islands sold to U.S.
Treaty of Versailles	1919	U.S. and other Allies' treaty with Germany following World War I, by which Germany ceded border territories and colonies, agreed to disarm and pay reparations, and League of Nations was created.
Nine-Power Treaty at the Washington Conference	1921-1922	U.S., Japan, Britain, France, and 5 other countries agreed to outlaw poison gas and respect China's integrity.
Kellogg-Briand Pact	1928	U.S. with Germany, Japan, and others agreed to outlaw war.
North Atlantic Treaty	1949	Established NATO
Treaty of Peace with Japan	1952	Treaty following World War II, by which Japan lost its conquests, agreed to help countries hurt during war, and was reconized as independent nation (49 signatures)
Southeast Asia Treaty Organization	1954	Established SEATO
Limited Nuclear Test Ban Treaty	1963	U.S., Britain, and Russia agreed not to test in atmosphere, space, or under water without onsite inspection
Nuclear Non-Proliferation Treaty	1968	U.S., Russia, and Britain with U.N. General Assembly, by which nations not having nuclear weapons agree not to develop them, effected 1970.
SALT I Accords	1972	U.S. and Russia agreed to limit ABM sites and to freeze size of offensive missile systems.
Panama Canal	1978	Canal returned to Panama
SALT II Treaty	1979	Proposed U.S. - Soviet ceiling on strategic nuclear delivery vehicles. (Not ratified by Senate.)
Intermediate Nuclear Force Treaty	1987	U.S. and Soviet Union agreed to begin dismantling intermediate range nuclear weapons.

92. American Media Firsts

Printing press in America (Cambridge)	1638
Successful newspaper: *Boston Newsletter*	1704
Daily newspaper: *Pennsylvania Packet and Daily Advertiser*	1784
Magazine in America: *The American Magazine*	1741
American novel (*The Pioneers*, James F. Cooper)	1823
American dictionary (Noah Webster)	1828
First journalism course (Washington University)	1869
Newspaper comic strip	1875
Book set by linotype	1886
Newspaper photograph	1890
Movie theater (New York City)	1894
Moving picture story: *The Great Train Robbery*	1903
Movie star (Max Aronson)	1903
Radio broadcast	1906
Animated cartoon: *Humorous Phases of Funny Faces*	1906
Female movie star (Florence Lawrence)	1907
Commercial radio station	1920
Play-by-play baseball game radio broadcast (Pittsburgh)	1921
Television receiver	1928
Color television demonstration	1929
Color talking picture: *On With the Show*	1929
Regular television broadcast made	1939
Commercial television station: WNBT, New York City	1941
National color television broadcast: *Colgate Comedy Hour*	1953
Videocassette recorders sold in United States	1976
FCC approves television broadcasting in stereo	1984

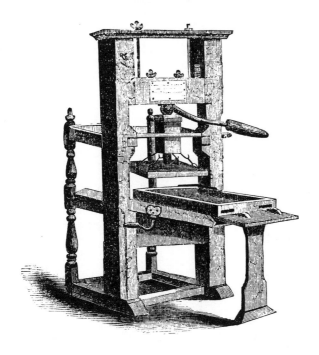

93. Slang of the 1970's

Slang	Meaning	Slang	Meaning
-aholic	suffix for any addiction	jive	nonsense
antsy	nervous	judgment call	a close choice
awesome	great	keep on truckin'	hang in there
biggie	important event or person	life style	way of life
boss	excellent	-mania	suffix for craze
burnout	exhausted from drugs, or stress	old fogey	old-fashioned person
bust	arrest for drug use	jock	any athlete
by the farm	to die	laid back	easy going
cheapie	low quality merchandise	match-up	a competition
come on like ganbusters	over-zealous	make waves	to cause trouble
		megabucks	large amount of money
cost an arm and a leg	expensive	narc	tattletale
decent	nice; very good	out-of-pocket	unreimbursed
dig	understand	preppy	dress like a prep school student
dirty pool	unfair tactics		
do a number on	try to deceive	punk	form of rock and roll
dork	a fool, nerd	right on	yes, that's right
down	bad experience	scuttlebutt	gossip
empowerment	taking control of one's life	shtick	act; show
		square one	beginning
even-handed	fair	step-by-step	in a sequence
fall guy	scapegoat	suave	well-poised
flea market	street sale	superstar	a major media idol
flat-out	totally	take care of business	to commence
flick	movie		
-gate	suffix for any scandal	totally awesome	wonderful!
get your act together	straighten out one's life	totally gross	disgusting
		track record	past achievements
get down	begin	trash	waste; destroy
get into	become interested	truck	walk
gig	job	turkey	a nerd
go bananas	get excited	up front	honest
gofer	lackey, errand runner	WASP	white, Anglo-Saxon, protestant
hang-up	a mental or emotional resistance		
		whole nine yards	full commitment; all the way
hassle	to annoy		
hatchet man	one brought in to fire employees	widget	mechanical contraption
head up	to lead; organize	workaholic	person compelled to work
humongous	very large		
hype	big promotional effort	zit	pimple
jet set	the super-wealthy		

94. Fads and Fancies of the 1970's

afro's (haircut)
backgammon
Ben Franklin glasses
bean bag chairs
bell bottom pants
bib overalls
biorhythms
CB's
chokers
"chopper" bicycles
clacker balls
Cuban heels on men's shoes
cybernetics
denim jackets
disco dancing
dreadlocks
earth shoes
8-track tapes
Farrah Fawcett-Majors posters
55 miles per hour speed limit
frizzy hair
flip-flops
G.I. fatigues
gypsy look
hang-gliding
headbands
health food stores
hot pants
hot tubs
Indian jewelry
"Jaws" T-shirts at the beach
jogging outfits
kissathon
macramé
maxi-skirt
mechanics' jump suits
mood rings
mutton chop sideburns

peace symbol
pet rocks
pie killing
puka shell necklaces
punk fashions
punk purple hair
roller disco
skateparks
"Space Invaders" video game
spandex garments
streaking
string bikinis
Susan B. Anthony dollar
Tarot
tattoos
think tanks
toga parties
"Trekkies"
unisex look
velveteen jackets
waterbeds
white stockings
wigs

95. Political Assassinations

Abraham Lincoln	President	1865
Charles Caldwell	Black Senator from Mississippi	1875
James Garfield	President	1881
William Goebel	Kentucky gubernatorial candidate	1900
William McKinley	President	1901
Huey P. Long	Louisiana Senator	1935
Medgar Evers	NAACP field representative	1963
John F. Kennedy	President	1963
Malcolm X	Black spokesman	1965
George Lincoln Rockwell	founder, American Nazi Party	1967
Martin Luther King, Jr.	civil rights leader	1968
Robert Kennedy	Attorney General of U.S.	1968
John Gorden Mein	U.S. Ambassador to Guatemala	1968
Joseph Yablonski	labor leader	1970
Leo Ryan	U.S. Representative	1978
George Mosone	Mayor of San Francisco	1978
Harvey Milk	San Francisco board of supervisors	1978
Adolph Dubs	U.S. Ambassador to Afghanistan	1979

96. Unsuccessful Presidential Assassinations

Theodore Roosevelt	1912
Franklin D. Roosevelt	1933
Harry S. Truman	1950
Gerald Ford	1975
Ronald Reagan	1981

97. Nicknames of Famous Americans

Sam Adams	Father of American Revolution
John James Audubon	American Woodsman
P. T. Barnum	Greatest Showman on Earth
Clara Barton	Angel of the Battlefield
Chuck Berry	Father of Rock and Roll
James G. Blaine	The Plumed Knight
William H. Bonney	Billy the Kid
Daniel Boone	Long Knife
Omar Bradley	Doughboy's General
William Jennings Bryan	The Peerless Leader of the Democratic Party
John C. Calhoun	Father of States' Rights; Onslow
Wilton Chamberlain	Wilt the Stilt
Lon Chaney	Man of a Thousand Faces
Charles Chaplin	The Little Tramp
John Chapman	Johnny Appleseed
Henry Clay	The Great Pacificator
Samiel Langhorne Clemens	Mark Twain
William F. Cody	Buffalo Bill
Stephen Douglas	The Little Giant
Thomas Edison	Wizard of Menlo Park
Adm. David Farragut	Hero of Mobile Bay
Benjamin Franklin	The American Socrates
Lou Gehrig	The Iron Mask
Ernest Hemingway	Papa
James Butler Hickock	Wild Bill Hickock
Gen. Joseph E. Hooker	Fighting Joe
Sam Houston	Father of Texas
Washington Irving	Diedrich Knickerbocker
Claudia Johnson	Lady Bird
Mary Harris Jones	Mother Jones
Cherilyn LaPiere	Cher
Henry Lee	Lighthorse Harry
Robert E. Lee	Uncle Robert
Jenny Lind	The Swedish Nightingale
Charles Lindberg	Lucky Lindy; Lone Eagle
Henry P. Long	The Kingfish
Gen. George McClellan	Little Mac
John Naismith	Father of Basketball
Thomas Paine	Humanus
Gen. George Patton	Old Blood and Guts
Gen. John J. Pershing	Blackjack Pershing
Elvis Presley	The King; The Pelvis
George Herman Ruth	Babe Ruth
Gen. Norman Schwarzkopf	Stormin' Norman
Gen. Winfield Scott	Old Fuss and Feathers
Gen. William T. Sherman	Old Tecump
Al Smith	The Happy Warrior
Harriet Tubman	Moses

98. Mottos

Join or die.
Liberty or death.
No taxation without representation.
Liberty and no excise.
Free trade and sailors' rights.
Millions for defense but not one cent for tribute.
In God we trust.
Remember the Alamo.
Fifty-four Forty or Fight.
California or Bust.
Death before Dishonor.
Remember the Maine.
Loose lips sink ships.
The war to end all wars.
Better dead than Red.
America, love it or leave it.
WIN (Whip Inflation Now)
Just say no.

99. Movies of Ronald Reagan

Accidents Will Happen
An Angel from Texas
Angels Wash Their Faces
The Bad Man
Bedtime for Bonzo
Boy Meets Girl
Brother Rat
Brother Rat and a Baby
Cattle Queen of Montana
Code of the Secret Service
Cowboy from Brooklyn
Dark Victory
Desperate Johnny
The Girl from Jones Beach
Girls on Probation
Going Places
The Hasty Heart
Hellcats of the Navy
Hell's Kitchen
Hollywood Hotel
Hong Kong
International Squadron
It's a Great Feeling
John Loves Mary
Juke Girl
The Killers

Kings Row
Knute Rockne—All American
The Last Outpost
Law and Order
Louisa
Love is on the Air
Million Dollar Baby
Murder in the Air
Naughty but Nice
Night Unto Night
Nine Lives Are Not Enough
Prisoner of War
Santa Fe Trail
Secret Service of the Air
Sergeant Murphy
She's Working Her Way Through College
Smashing the Money Ring
Stallion Road
Storm Warning
Swing Your Lady
Tennessee's Partner
That Hagen Girl
This Is the Army
Tugboat Annie Sails Again
The Voice of the Turtle
The Winning Team
Tropic Zone

100. Slang of the 80's

Term	Meaning
beltway bandit	Washington, D.C. consultant
bean counter	numbers person, accountant
boom box	large portable radio
bow heads	girls wearing ribbons
break dance	style of gymnastic dance
CD	compact disk
casual	fashionable, good
chill	calm down
clonked out	broken
Clydesdale	handsome guy
couch potato	persistent television viewer
dancercise	aerobics to music
ditsy	flaky
dude	guy, man
dweeb	nerd
fast-tracker	person moving up the corporate ladder
fine tune	to adjust, perfect
floppies	computer disks
freezenik	person for a nuclear freeze
fresh	cool, nice
fuzzify	to muddle
gag me with a spoon	disgusting!
ghetto blaster	a big portable radio
go for it	try it
golden parachute	big severance pay agreement for executives of companies merging
groovy	old fashioned
hacker	one who breaks into computer files
hands-on manager	boss who gets directly involved
happening	an important event
happy camper	satisfied person
have a cow	get excited, over-react
house	to steal
I'm so sure.	Right (sarcastically)
major league	important
make a run for the border	skip school
make my day	don't mess with me
maxed out	credit cards charged to the limit
networking	using personal contacts for career gain
PC	personal computer
photo op	chance for pictures of a politician
plastic	phony
power tie	dress for success necktie
prioritizing	establishing priorities
proactive	taking preventative action
quality time	giving attention to loved ones

100. Slang of the 80's, continued

Term	Meaning
radical	outstanding; excellent
rank	good looking
red eye	late night flight
rock-jock	a mountain climber
slammin'	enjoyable
sound bite	political quote for television broadcast
streamlining	making more aero-dynamic, simplifying
stretch	a long limo
totally gross	disgusting!
twisted grill	crooked teeth
VJ	video jockey
up-scale marketing	advertising targeted at wealthy consumers
upside potential	opportunity for a profit
verbal	to harass, rib
What's shakin'?	What's happening?
Where's the beef?	Where's the result?
yo	hey; hello
YUPPIE	young urban professional
zapping	using fast forward on VCR to skip commercials
zedwig	nerd

101. Innovations of the 80's

airbags
answering machines
autofocus cameras
automatic teller machines
BMX bicycles
boombox
cable television
cable TV shopping
call forwarding
call waiting
camcorders
cellular telephones
compact discs
computer spelling checkers
cordless telephones
curb recycling
disposable cameras
electronic mail
EPCOT
fax machines
food processors
frequent flyer programs
front wheel drive cars
frozen yogurt
gourmet frozen dinners
hair mousse
home computers
junk bonds
laser discs
laser printers
liposuction

"Lite" everything
living wills
microcassette
microwave ovens
miniature portable televisions
minivans
modems
mouse (computer control)
mandatory seat belt laws
New Coke
Nintendo
nursery monitors
911 emergency phone service
non-smoking
patriot missiles
personal computers
Post-it notes
quality circles
radar detectors
return of the 65 mph speed limit
solar calculators
space shuttle
stealth bombers
space telescope
state lotteries
tomahawk missiles
unisex clothing
universal bar code
voice mail
Walkman
wireless remote control

102. First Blacks

First Black . . .

child born in America	William Tucker	1621
founder of Chicago	Jean Baptiste du Sable	1772
poet	Phillis Wheatley	1774
presidential appointee	Benjamin Banneker	1791
black minister of a white congregation	John Morront	1795
bishop in the U.S.	Richard Allen	1816
college graduate	John Russwurm	1826
patent holder	Henry Blair	1834
to publish a novel	W. W. Brown	1853
elected to an office	John Mercer	1854
chaplin of U.S. Army	Henry M. Turner	1863
major in U.S. Army	Martin Delany	1865
United States senator	Hiram Rhodes Revels	1870
Kentucky derby winner	Oliver Lewis	1875
Ph.D. recipient (Yale)	E.A. Bouchet	1876
baseball player	Moses Fleetwood	1883
professional baseball team	Cuban Giants	1884
millionaire	Jonathan Wright	1885
Harvard Ph.D. recipient	W.E.B. Du Bois	1895
rodeo bulldogger	Bill Pickett	1900
Medal of Honor winner	William Harvey Carney	1900
female bank president	Lena Walker	1902
sorority	Alpha Kappa Alpha	1908
heavyweight champion	Jack Johnson	1908
set foot on North Pole	Matthew Henson	1909
Rhodes scholar	Alain Leroy Locke	1910
female millionaire	C.J. Walker	1914
All American football player	"Fritz" Pollard	1916
professional football player	"Fritz" Pollard	1919
basketball team	Renaissance	1923
woman state legislator	Crystal Fauset	1938
woman judge	Jane M. Bolin	1939
to perform at the White House	Marian Anderson	1939
Oscar winner	Hattie McDaniel	1940
to play in baseball major leagues	Jackie Robinson	1947
Naval academy graduate	Wesley Brown	1949
U.S. Naval pilot	Jessie Brown	1949
Pulitzer prize winner	Gwendolyn Brooks	1950
Nobel Peace prize winner	Dr. Ralph Bunche	1950
NBA basketball playre	Charles H. Cooper	1950
air force general	Benjamin O. Davis, Jr.	1954
Wimbleton competitor	Althea Gibson	1957
professional hockey player	Willie O'Ree	1958
airline stewardess	Ruth Carol Taylor	1958
Heisman trophy winner	Ernie Davis	1961
student at University of Mississippi	James Meredith	1962
warship commander	Samuel Gravely	1962
major league umpire	Emmett Ashford	1966

102. First Blacks, continued

Cabinet member	Robert C. Weaver	1966
on Federal Reserve Board of Governors	Andrew Brimmer	1966
Supreme Court justice	Thurgood Marshall	1967
professional sports coach	Bill Russell	1967
orchestra conductor	Henry Lewis	1968
professional football quarterback	Martin Briscoe	1968
woman in House of Representatives	Shirley Chisholm	1969
to win "Mr. America" contest	Chris Dickerson	1970
major league baseball manager	Frank Robinson	1975
woman armed services pilot	Loren Monroe	1979
to win "Miss America"	Vanessa Williams	1983
Texas Ranger	Lee Roy Young	1988
Roman Catholic archbishop	Eugene Marino	1988
chairman of Joint Chiefs of Staff	Gen. Colin Powell	1989
head of a major political party	Ronald Brown	1989

103. Sources for Genealogical Research

birth certificates
cemetery records
census records
church record
city directories
county histories
criminal records
death certificates
diaries
family Bibles
immigration records
land deeds
living relatives

marriage records
military records
naturalization records
newspaper files
probate court records
published family histories
school records
tax roles
telephone directories
tombstones
veteran pension records
wills

104. History-Oriented Periodicals

© 1992 by Prentice-Hall

American Heritage
American Historical Review
American History Illustrated
American Jewish Historical Review
American Quarterly
The America West
Art and Archaeology Newsletter
British Heritage
Canada West
Chicago History
Civil War Times Illustrated
Genealogical Helper
Historic Preservation
Indian Historian
Journal of American History
*Journal of Interdisciplinary
 History*

Journal of Southern History
Journal of the History of Ideas
Journal of Genealogy
*Mankind: The Magazine of Popular
 History*
Military Review
North Carolina Historical Review
North South Trader
Old West
Persimmon Hill
Social Education
Social Studies Review
*Theory and Research in Social
 Education*
True West
Virginia Cavalcade
*Virginia Magazine of History and
 Biography*
Wisconsin Magazine of History

Section II

LISTS FOR
WORLD HISTORY

105. Innovations and Contributions of Ancient Egypt

advertisements
books
bowling
bread
candy
checkers
clarinet
dice
domestic cats
embalming
football
gambling
ink
masonry
oboe
paper
papyrus
pens
postal system
sailing
sundial
tapestry
tunnel
water clocks

106. The Seven Wonders of the Ancient World

The Temple of Artemis at Euphesus on the west coast of present-day Turkey, was built around 550 B.C. Except for the wooden roof this massive temple was built entirely of marble. The ornately decorated temple was dedicated to the Greek goddess Artemis. The original temple was destroyed and rebuilt several times. In 262 A.D. Goths destroyed the final structure. Today only the foundation and parts of the second temple survive.

The State of Zeus at Olympia, Greece, was built around 435 B.C. by the sculptor Phidias. It was dedicated to the king of gods, Zeus. The 40 foot high statue depicted Zeus on a golden throne. His robe and ornaments were made of gold and his skin of ivory. It was probably destroyed by invading armies.

The Lighthouse of Alexandria, Egypt, was built during the reign of Ptolemy (283-246 B.C. on the island of Pharos. It rose approximately 440 feet. It stood on a massive platform of three sections; the bottom one was square, the middle octagonal, and the top circular. The fire at the top guided ships into the harbor for over a thousand years before it was brought down by an earthquake.

The Mausoleum at Halicarnassus was a massive marble tomb built for King Mausolus, a Persian Empire ruler who died in 353 B.C. Located in present-day southwestern Turkey it was built by his widow Artemisia, who was also his sister. The fame of the tomb provided the source of the term "mausoleum." While the tomb survived 1900 years, it was finally toppled by an earthquake.

The Colossus of Rhodes was erected at the Harbor of Rhodes on the Aegean Sea in the early 200's B.C. The huge bronze statue was built in honor of the sun god Helios. The hollow statue was built of stone blocks and iron support bars with thin copper plating. It stood 1200 feet tall. It was destroyed by an earthquake in 224 B.C. In 667 A.D. its remains were sold for scrap.

The Hanging Gardens of Babylon were built by King Nebuchadnezzar II near modern day Baghdad in Iraq. Historians speculate that the gardens were built by the king for one of his wives. The garden was laid out on a massive brick terrace approximately 400 feet square and 75 feet high. An elaborate irrigation system brought water from the Euphrates River.

The Pyramids of Egypt are the only Wonder of the Ancient World still standing. They were also the oldest of the Ancient Wonders. They were built as tombs for the Egyptian kings. One of the most famous of the pyramids is the Great Pyramid of Cheops built around 2600 B.C. It stands 4821 feet high near Cairo.

107. Authors of Ancient Greece

Aeschylus
Aristophanes
Demosthenes
Euripides
Herodotus
Homer
Plato
Sophocles
Thucydides

108. Authors of Ancient Rome

Cattullus
Cicero
Cato the Elder
Gaius Lucilius
Gnaeus Naevius
Horace
Julius Caesar
Juvenal
Livy
Lucan
Lucius Accius
Lucius Aurelius
Lucretius
Marcus Aurelius
Martial
Marcus Pacuvius
Ovid
Pliny the Elder
Quintus Ennius
Sallust
Seneca
Tacitus
Varro
Virgil

109. Innovations and Contributions of Ancient Sumer

adoption
drug catalog
elementary schools
harp
jacks (game)
jewelry
literature
pear

schools
theater
tuition
universities
wheel
wheeled vehicles
writing

110. Innovations and Contributions of Ancient Greece

Archimedean screw
boxing
column
drama
encyclopedia
geometry
libraries

lighthouses
mime
mosaic floors
philosophy
public education
sculpture
shorthand

111. Ancient Units of Measurement

cubit	length of a man's arm (20.5")
digit	width of a finger (28 digits = 1 cubit)
palm	4 digits
hand	5 digits
t'ser	4 palms
foot	16 fingers
inch	width of a man's thumb
foot	length of a man's foot
yard	distance from a man's nose to the tip of his middle finger
dinar	.15 ounce (Arabia)
stadium	606 feet
drachma	.154 ounces
mina	100 drachmas
swan	100 minas
shekel	about 1/2 oz.
amphora	6.84 gallons (Rome)
ephah	1.1 bushels

112. Hebrew Months

Tishri (September-October)
Heshvan, or Marheshvan (October-November)
Kislev (November-December)
Tevet (December-January)
Shevat (January-February)
Adar (February-March)
Nisan (March-April)
Iyyar (April-May)
Sivan (May-June)
Temmuz (June-July)
Av (July-August)
Elul (August-September)

113. Jewish Holidays

Pesah	(Passover)
Shavuos	(Pentecost)
Tisha bAv	(Ninth of Av)
Rosh Hashana	(New Year)
Yom Kippur	(Day of Atonement)
Sukkot	(Tabernacles)
Hanukka	(Feast of Dedication)
Purim	(Feast of Lots)

114. The Ten Commandments

1. I am the Lord your God.
2. You shall take no other gods before me. You shall not make for yourself a sculptured image . . .
3. You shall not swear falsely by name of the Lord your God . . .
4. Remember the sabbath and keep it holy . . .
5. Honor your father and mother . . .
6. You shall not murder.
7. You shall not commit adultry.
8. You shall not steal.
9. You should not bear false witness against your neighbor.
10. You should not covet your neighbor's house or wife or anything that is your neighbors.

115. The Seven Deadly Sins

avarice
pride
wrath
lust
gluttony
sloth
envy

116. Innovations and Contributions of Ancient Rome

bilingual education
circus
concrete
Julian calendar
newspapers

one-way streets
paved roads
state-supported schools
stone bridges
stop signs

117. Roman Numerals

1	I	80	LXXX
2	II	90	XC
3	III	100	C
4	IV	200	CC
5	V	300	CCC
6	VI	400	CD
7	VII	500	D
8	VIII	600	DC
9	IX	700	DCC
10	X	800	DCCC
11	XI	900	CM
12	XII	1,000	M
13	XIII	1,100	MC
14	XIV	1,200	MCC
15	XV	1,300	MCCC
16	XVI	1,400	MCD
17	XVII	1,500	MD
18	XVIII	2,000	MM
19	XIX	2,100	MMC
20	XX	3,000	MMM
30	XXX	4,000	$M\overline{V}$
40	XL	5,000	$\overline{V}$
50	L	10,000	$\overline{X}$
60	LX	20,000	$\overline{XX}$
70	LXX	50,000	$\overline{L}$
		100,000	$\overline{C}$
		500,000	$\overline{D}$
		1,000,000	$\overline{M}$

118. Nicknames of Various World Leaders

Nickname	Name
Almighty Nose	Oliver Cromwell
Badinguet	Napoleon III
Bloody Mary	Queen Mary I of England
Boney	Napoleon Bonaparte
Chairman Mao	Mao Tse-tung
Citizen King	King Louis Philippe
Conqueror, The	William I of England
Der Führer	Adolph Hitler
Desert Fox	Erwin Rommel
Devil's Missionary, The	Voltaire
Divine Madman	Michelangelo
Dizzy	Benjamin Disraeli
El Libertador	Simon Bolivar
Gentleman Johnny	British Gen. John Burgoyne
Goldy	Oliver Goldsmith
Good Queen Bess	Queen Elizabeth I of England
Grand Old Man	William Gladstone
Great Commoner	William Pitt
Great Helmsman	Mao Tse-tung
Last of the Puritans	Samuel Adams
Little Corporal	Napoleon Bonaparte
Iberia's Pilot	Christopher Columbus
Iron Chancellor	Otto von Bismarck
Iron Duke	Duke of Wellington
Iron Lady	Margaret Thatcher
Knight of the Cloak	Sir Walter Raleigh
Lady With a Lamp	Florence Nightingale
Liberator, The	Simon Bolivar
Lenin, Nikolai	Vladimir Ilich Ulyanov
Lion Heart	King Richard I
Old Noll	Oliver Cromwell
Orange Peel	Sir Robert Peel
Peacemaker	King Edward VII
Philosopher, The	Aristotle
Scourge of God	Attila the Hun
Tiger, The	George B. Clemenceau

119. The Greek Alphabet

alpha	A	α
beta	B	β
gamma	Γ	γ
delta	Δ	δ
epsilon	E	ε
zeta	Z	ζ
eta	H	η
theta	Θ	θ
iota	I	ι
kappa	K	κ
lamda	Λ	λ
mu	M	μ
nu	N	ν
xi	Ξ	ξ
omicron	O	ο
pi	Π	π
rho	P	ρ
sigma	Σ	σ
tau	T	τ
upsilon	Y	υ
phi	Φ	φ
chi	X	χ
psi	Ψ	ψ
omega	Ω	ω

120. Fathers of . . .

America	Samuel Adams, colonial patriot
Comedy	Aristophanes, Greek writer of comedy
The Constitution	James Madison, author of the U.S. Constitution
English Poetry	Geoffrey Chaucer, author of *Canterbury Tales*
The Faithful	Abraham, founder of the Hebrew race
His Country	George Washington, first President of the United States
History	Herodotus, Greek historian
Medicine	Hippocrates, famous Greek physician
Philosophy	Roger Bacon, English philosopher
Roman Philosophy	Cicero, Roman philosopher and orator
Satire	Archilochus, Greek poet
The Symphony	Joseph Haydn, Austrian composer

121. Romance Languages

French
Italian
Portuguese
Romanian
Spanish

122. Major Egyptian Deities

Amon	king of the gods
Anubis	god of the dead
Geb	god of the earth
Horus	god of heaven and light
Isis	Mother of all things
Ptah	god of fertility
Re or Ra	sun god, ruler of the world
Set	god of evil; god of the desert
Shu	god of light, air, supporter of the sky
Thoth	moon god; god of learning and wisdom

123. Greek Deities

Aeolus	gods of the winds
Aesculapius	god of healing
Aphrodite	goddess of love
Apollo	god of music, purity, and poetry
Ares	god of war
Artemis	goddess of hunting and childbirth
Asclepius	god of healing
Athena	goddess of wisdom and war
Chloris	goddess of flowers
Cronus	ruler of the Titans
Demeter	goddess of growing things
Dionysus	god of wine, fertility, and wild behavior
Eros	god of love
Eris	goddess of strife and discord
Hades	god of the underworld
Hephaestus	god of fire
Hermes	god of commerce and science
Hestia	goddess of the hearth
Hygeia	goddess of health
Hypnos	god of sleep
Morpheus	god of dreams
Nemesis	goddess of vengeance
Nike	goddess of victory
Nyx	goddess of night
Pan	god of the forest and pastures
Plutus	god of wealth
Poseidon	god of the sea, horses, and earthquakes
Rhea	mother of the Olympian goddesses and gods
Selene	goddess of the moon
Thantos	god of death
Uranus	god of heaven
Zeus	ruler of heaven; chief of the deities

124. Roman Deities

Aurora	goddess of the dawn
Bacchus	god of wine, fertility, and wild behavior
Ceres	goddess of growing things
Coelus	god of heaven
Cupid	god of love
Diana	goddess of hunting and childbirth
Dis	god of the underworld
Faunus	god of fields and shepherds
Janus	god of entryways
Juno	queen of the gods; Jupiter's wife
Jupiter	ruler of the gods
Juventas	goddess of youth
Luna	goddess of the moon
Mars	god of war
Mercury	god of commerce and science
Minerva	goddess of crafts, war, and wisdom
Mors	god of death
Neptune	god of the sea
Nox	god of night
Picus	god who foretold the future
Pluto	god of the underworld
Pomona	goddess of fruits and trees
Psyche	goddess of the soul
Salacia	goddess of the oceans
Saturn	god of agriculture
Somnus	god of sleep
Terminus	god of boundries
Tiberinus	god of the Tiber River
Venus	goddess of love
Vesta	goddess of the hearth
Victoria	goddess of victory
Vulcan	god of fire

125. Major Wars

War	Dates
Peloponnesian War	431-404 B.C.
Punic Wars	264-146 B.C.
Crusades	1096-1291
Hundred Years War	1337-1453
War of the Roses	1455-1485
Thirty Years' War	1618-1648
French and Indian Wars	1689-1763
Seven Years' Wars	1756-1763
American Revolution	1775-1783
French Revolution	1789-1799
War of 1812	1812-1814
Mexican War	1846-1848
Revolution of 1848	1848
Crimean War	1853-1856
U.S. Civil War	1861-1865
Franco-Prussian War	1870
First Anglo-Boer War	1880-1881
Chinese-Japanese War	1894-1895
Spanish-American War	1898
Second Anglo-Boer War	1904-1905
Russo-Japanese War	1904-1905
Russian Revolution	1905
World War I	1914-1918
Russian Revolution	1917
World War II	1939-1945
Arab-Israeli Wars	1948, 1956, 1967, 1973
Korean War	1950-1953
Vietnam War	1957-1975
Persian Gulf War	1991

126. Early Weapons

articulated clubs	gauntlets
axes	halberds
blowgun	maces
boomerangs	rapiers
bow and arrow	sling shots
catapult	spears
chakram	swords
clubs	throwing clubs
crossbow	tomahawk
daggers	war hammers
flails	whips

127. Major Indian Tribes of Latin America

Araucanian
Arawak
Aztec
CaribChibcha
Gê
Inca
Jívaro
Maya
Olmec
Ona
Tarascan
Toltec
Tupí-Guaraní
Zapotec

128. "Hello" in Other Languages

Czech	pozdroav
French	bonjour
German	hallo
Italian	olà
Polish	halo
Portuguese	alô
Spanish	¡hola!
Svensk	hallå!
Swahili	maamkio

129. "Peace" in Other Languages

Czech	mir, pokoj
French	paix
Gaelic	tosd!
German	der Friede
Italian	pace
Latin	pax
Polish	pokoju, spokój
Portuguese	paz
Spanish	paz
Svensk	frid
Swahili	amani

130. "Love" in Other Languages

Czech	milovati
French	amour
German	die Liebe
Gaelic	gradhaich
Italian	amore
Latin	amor
Portuguese	amor
Spanish	amar
Swahili	upendo

131. Major Languages of the World

Arabic
Bengali
Cantonese
English
French
German
Hindi
Italian
Japanese
Javanese
Korean
Malay-Indonesian
Mandarin
Portuguese
Russian
Spanish
Tamil
Telugu
Thai
Turkish
Ukranian
Urdu
Vietnamese
Wu

132. British Positions of Title

King	Queen
Prince of Wales	Princess of Wales
Duke	Duchess
Prince	Princess
Marquess	Marchioness
Earl	Countess
Viscount	Viscountess
Baron	Baroness
Life Baron	Life Baroness
Baronet	Baronetess
Knight	Dame
Lord of the Manor	Lady of the Manor

133. Contributions and Innovations of China

brandy
cast iron
chess
collar harness
compass
cannon
cross bow
decimal mathematics
drive belt
fireworks
fishing reel
flame thrower
grenades
gun powder
guns
hot air balloon
immunology
iron plowshare
kite
lacquer
liquor
Mandarin orange
mechanical clock
moldboard plow
mortars
multi-stage rocket

negative numbers
paddle wheel
paper
paper money
parachutes
playing cards
poison gas
porcelain
printing
relief maps
rocket
rotary fan
row planting
seed drill
seismograph
ship's rudder
sliding caliper
soybean
spinning wheel
stirrup
suspension bridge
tea
tear gas
umbrella
underwater mine
water power
wheelbarrow
whiskey

134. The Signs of the Zodiac

Capricorn	goat	Dec. 22 - Jan 19
Aquarius	water bearer	Jan. 20 - Feb 18
Pisces	fishes	Feb. 19 - Mar. 20
Aries	ram	March 21 - Apr. 19
Taurus	bull	Apr. 20 - May 20
Gemini	twins	May 21 - June 20
Cancer	crab	June 21 - July 22
Leo	lion	July 23 - Aug. 22
Virgo	virgin	Aug. 23 - Sept. 22
Libra	scales	Sept. 23 - Oct. 22
Scorpio	scorpion	Oct. 23 - Nov. 21
Sagittarius	archer	Nov. 22 - Dec. 21

135. Names of the Months

January	named after Janus, Roman god of entryways
February	from Februa, the Latin festival of purification celebrated on February 15
March	named for Mars, the Roman god of war
April	from *aperire*, Latin word for "to open"
May	derived from maiores, Latin for "elders." Romans honored the elderly during this month.
June	either from Juno, the Roman queen of the goddesses, or from *juniores*, Latin for "youngsters"
July	named in honor of Julius Caesar
August	named in honor of Roman emperor, Augustus Caesar
September	from *septem*, Latin for seven. This was the seventh month in the Roman calendar.
October	from *octo*, Latin for eight
November	from *novem*, Latin for nine
December	from *decem*, Latin for ten

136. The Days of the Week

Sunday	from *Solis Dies*, Latin for "sun's day"
Monday	from *Monan Dæg*, Anglo-Saxon for "moon's day"
Tuesday	from *Tiwes Dæg*, Anglo-Saxon form for Tyr, Norse god of war
Wednesday	from *Wodnes Dæg*, Anglo-Saxon spelling of Odin, the Norse god of war and victory
Thursday	from Thueres Dæg, after Thor, the Norse god of thunder
Friday	from Friges Dæg, after the Norse goddess of love, Frigg
Saturday	named for the Latin god, Saturn

137. Early Explorers of the Americas

982	Eric the Red	off coast of Canada
1000	Leif Ericson	Newfoundland (?)
1492	Christopher Columbus	Carribean Islands
1497	John Cabot	Nova Scotia or Newfoundland
1498	John and Sebastian Cabot	North American coast
1499	Amerigo Vespucci	South America & West Indies
1499	Alonso de Ojeda	South American coast
1500	Vincent y Pinzon	Amazon River
1500	Pedro Alvares Cabral	Brazil
1513	Vasco Nunex de Balboa	Pacific Ocean
1513	Juan Ponce de Leon	Florida
1519	Alonso de Pineda	Mississippi River delta
1519	Hernando Cortés	Mexico
1520	Ferdinand Magellan	Tierra del Fuego, Straits of Magellan
1524	Giovanni da Verrazano	North American east coast
1532	Francisco Pizarro	Peru
1534	Jacques Cartier	Canada
1536	Cabeza de Vaca	inland Texas
1539	Francisco do Ulloa	California coast
1539	Hernando de Soto	Mississippi River
1540	Francisco V. de Coronado	U.S. southwest
1540	Hernando Alarcon	Colorado River
1541	Francisco de Orellana	Amazon River
1565	Pedro Menendez de Aviles	St. Augustine
1576	Martin Frobisher	Frobisher's Bay, Canada
1577	Frances Draker	California coast
1585	Sir Walter Raleigh's men	Outer Banks, North Carolina
1598	Juan de Oñate	American southwest
1603	Samuel de Champlain	Lake Champlain, Canada
1607	John Smith	Atlantic coast
1609	Henry Hudson	Hudson Bay, Hudson River
1634	Jean Nicolet	Wisconsin, Lake Michigan
1673	Louis Jolliet, Jacques Marquette	Mississippi River
1679	Louis Hennepin	upper Mississippi River
1682	Sieur de La Salle	Mississippi River
1731	Pierre Gaultier de Varennes	Saskatchewan

138. The Allies of World War I

Belgium
Brazil
British Empire
China
Costa Rica
Cuba
France
Greece
Guatemala
Haiti
Honduras
Italy
Japan

Liberia
Montenegro
Nicaragua
Panama
Romania
Russia
San Marino
Serbia
Siam
United States

139. The Central Powers

Austria-Hungary
Bulgaria
Germany
Ottoman Empire

140. Battle Casualties of World War I

Russia	1,700,000
German	1,600,000
France	1,385,300
Great Britain	900,000
Austria	800,000
Italy	460,000
Serbia	325,000
Turkey	250,000
Belgium	102,000
Romania	100,000
United States	67,813
Bulgaria	46,000
Greece	7,000
Montenegro	3,000
Portugal	2,000

141. Allies of World War II

Argentina	Iran
Australia	Iraq
Belgium	Lebanon
Bolivia	Liberia
Brazil	Luxembourg
Canada	Mexico
China	Mongolian People's Republic
Columbia	Netherlands
Costa Rica	New Zealand
Cuba	Nicaragua
Czechoslovakia	Norway
Denmark	Panama
Dominican Republic	Paraguay
Ecuador	Peru
Egypt	Poland
El Salvador	Russia
Ethiopia	Saudi Arabia
France	South Africa
Great Britain	Syria
Greece	Turkey
Guatemala	United States
Haiti	Uruguay
Honduras	Venezuela
India	Yugoslavia

142. Allies' Military Leaders of World War II

Harold Alexander	George C. Marshall
Henry Arnold	Andrew McNaughton
Omar Bradley	Bernard Montgomery
Claire Chennault	Louis Mountbatten
Mark Clark	Chester Nimitz
Lucius Clay	George S. Patton, Jr.
James Doolittle	Matthew Ridgeway
Dwight D. Eisenhower	Joseph Stilwell
William Halsey, Jr.	Maxwell Taylor
Oveta Hobby	Jonathan Wainwright
Ernest King	Archibald Wavell
William Leahy	Georgi Zhukov
Curtis LeMay	
Douglas MacArthur	

143. The Axis Powers

Albania	Italy
Bulgaria	Japan
Finland	Romania
Germany	Thailand
Hungary	

144. Axis Military Leaders

Karl Doenitz
Hermann Goering
Reinhard Heyddrich
Alfred Jodl
Wilhelm Keitel
Erwin Rommel
Isoruku Yamamoto
Tomobumi Yamashita

145. Authors Whose Books Were Burned by the Nazis

In May of 1933 massive book burnings were conducted throughout Germany by the Nazis. The following authors were among those whose books were burned:

Alfred Adler	Jack London
Albert Einstein	Heinrich Mann
Sigmund Freud	Thomas Mann
Maxim Gorki	Karl Marx
Heinrich Heine	Marcel Proust
Ernest Hemingway	Upton Sinclair
Helen Keller	Leon Trotsky
Nikolai Lenin	

146. Weapons of World War II

aerial bombs
aircraft cannon
anti-craft guns
assault weapons
atomic bombs
bayonets
bazookas
daggers
depth charges
explosives
field artillery
hand grenades
flamethrower
incendiary bombs

land mines
machine guns
mortors
naval guns
naval mines
revolvers
recoilless rifles
rifle grenades
rifles
rockets
semi-automatic pistols
sub-machine guns
V 2 rocket

147. Major Confrontations of World War II

Dunkirk
Battle of Britain
Moscow
Malta
Sinking of the Bismarck
Midway
Guadalcanal
El Alamein
Stalingrad
Kursk
Anzio/Cassino
Kohima/Imphal
The Normandy Invasion
Arnhem
Battle of the Bulge
Berlin
Okinawa

148. Original Members of the United Nations (1945)

Argentina
Australia
Belgium
Bolivia
Brazil
Byelorussian Soviet
  Socialist Republic
Canada
Chile
China
Columbia
Costa Rica
Cuba
Czechoslovakia
Denmark
Dominican Republic
Ecquador
Egypt
El Salvador
Ethiopia
France
Greece
Guatemala
Haiti
Honduras
India

Iran
Iraq
Lebanon
Liberia
Luxembourg
Mexico
Netherlands
New Zealand
Nicaragua
Norway
Panama
Paraguay
Peru
Philippines
Poland
Saudi Arabia
South Africa
Syria
Turkey
Ukrainian Soviet Socialist Republic
Union of Soviet Socialist Republics
United Kingdom
United States
Uruguay
Venezuela
Yugoslavia

149. Agencies of the United Nations

General Agreement on Tariffs and Trade (GATT)
Food and Agriculture Organization (FAO)
International Atomic Energy Agency (IAEA)
International Bank for Reconstruction and Development (World Bank)
International Civil Aviation Organization (ICAO)
International Development Association (IDA)
International Finance Corporation (IFC)
International Fund for Agricultural Development (IFAD)
International Labor Organization (ILO)
International Marine Organization (IMO)
International Monetary Fund (IMF)
International Telecommunication Union (ITU)
United Nations Educational, Scientifc and Cultural Organization (UNESCO)
United Nations Industrial Development Organization (UNIDO)
Universal Postal Union (UPU)
World Health Organization (WHO)
World Intellectual Property Organization (WIPO)
World Meterological Organization (WMO)

150. United Nations Secretaries General

Secretary General	Country	Elected
Trygve Lie	Norway	1946
Dag Hammarskjold	Sweden	1953
U Thant	Burma	1961
Kurt Waldheim	Austria	1972
Javier Perez de Cuellar	Peru	1982
Boutros Ghali	Egypt	1992

151. Political Assassinations of Modern Times

Victim	Position	Year
Abraham Lincoln	President of the U.S.	1865
Justo Jose de Urquiza	President of Argentina	1870
James Garfield	President of the U.S.	1881
William McKinley	President of the U.S.	1901
Butrus Pasha Ghali	Primier of Egypt	1910
Peter Arkadevich Stolypin	Prime Minister of Russia	1911
Frances Ferdinand	Archduke of Austria	1914
Grigori Rasputin	Advisor to Russian Czar	1916
Nicholas II & family	Czar of Russia	1918
Emiliano Zapata	Mexican revolutionary	1919
Alexander I	King of Yugoslavia	1934
Leon Trotsky	Russian revolutionary	1934
Benito Mussolini	Italian dictator	1945
Mohandas Ghandi	Nationalist of India	1948
Ngo Dinh Dien	President of Vietnam	1963
John F. Kennedy	President of U.S.	1963
Malcolm X	Black spokesman	1965
Robert Kennedy	Attorney General of U.S.	1968
Martin Luther King	U.S. civil rights leader	1968
Zulfikar Bhutto	Ex-prime minister of Pakistan	1979
Louis Mountbatten	Earl of Burma	1979
Anwar Sadat	President of Egypt	1981
Benigno Aquino, Jr.	Philippine politician	1983
Indira Ghandi	Prime Minister of India	1984
Rajiv Ghandi	Former Prime Minister of India	1991

152. Voter Participation by Country
(From most recent national elections)

Rank	Country	Turnout *(As percentage of electorate)*
1	Australia	94.17%
2	New Zealand	93.71%
3	Belgium	93.59%
4	Austria	92.59%
5	Turkey	92.27%
6	Sweden	89.85%
7	Germany	89.09%
8	Italy	89.00%
9	Iceland	88.60%
10	Denmark	88.44%
11	Venezuela	87.75%
12	Netherlands	85.70%
13	Norway	81.21%
14	Luxembourg	80.60%
15	Greece	80.19%
16	Spain	80.18%
17	Israel	78.78%
18	France	78.29%
19	Finland	75.73%
20	Canada	75.66%
21	Ireland	72.86%
22	Great Britain	72.86%
23	Japan	67.94%
24	India	63.53%
25	Switzerland	48.91%
26	United States	48.70%

Source: The Congressional Research Service as reported in *The National Voter*. (1989) 38:5, p. 2 (Used with permission)

Election returns from all countries except the United States were obtained from Inter-Parliamentary Union, Chronicle of Parliamentary Elections, International Centre for Parliamentary Documentation. Election returns for the United States were compiled by Election Data Services, Inc., Washington D.C.

153. Republics of the U.S.S.R.

Armenia
Azerbaijan
Byelorussia
Estonia
Georgia
Kazakhstan
Kirghizia
Latvia
Lithuania
Moldavia
Russia
Tadzhikistan
Turkmenistan
Uzbekistan
Ukraine

154. Languages of the U.S.S.R.

Armenian
Avar
Azerbaijani
Bashkir
Belorussian
Buryat
Chechen
Chukchi
Chuvash
Evenki
Estonian
Georgian
Kabardian
Kazakh
Kirgiz
Komi

Lalmyk
Latvian
Lithuanian
Mari
Mordvin
Nenets
Ossetian
Ostyak
Russian
Tadzhik
Tatar
Turkmen
Udmurt
Ukrainian
Uzbek
Yakut

155. Languages of Europe

Albanian	Italian
Basque	Lappish
Breton	Latin
Bulgarian	Luxembourgian
Catalan	Macedonian
Croatian	Norwegian
Czech	Polish
Danish	Portuguese
Dutch	Provencal
English	Rhaeto-Romanic
Faroese	Romany
Finnish	Rumanian
Flemish	Serbian
French	Slovak
Frisian	Slovenian
Gaelic	Sorbian
German	Spanish
Greek	Swedish
Hungarian	Welsh
Icelandic	Yiddish

156. Members of the European Economic Community

Belgium
Denmark
France
Germany
Ireland
Italy
Luxembourg
Netherlands
United Kingdom

157. 1980's Nobel Peace Prize Winners

1990	Mikhail Gorbachev, U.S.S.R.
1989	Dalai Lama, Leader of Tibet
1988	United Nations Peacekeeping Forces
1987	Oscar Arias Sanchez, Costa Rica
1986	Elie Wiesel, Rumania-United States
1985	Int'l. Physicians for the Prevention of Nuclear War, United States
1984	Bishop Desmond Tutu, South Africa
1983	Lech Walesa, Poland
1982	Alva Myrdal, Sweden & Alfonso Garcia Robles, Mexico
1981	Office of United Nations High Commission for Refugees
1980	Adolfo Perez Esquivel, Argentina

158. Sites of the Modern Olympic Games

Summer Games		**Winter Games**
1896	Athens	
1900	Paris	
1904	St, Louis	
1908	London	
1912	Stockholm	
1916	World War I	
1920	Antwerp	
1924	Paris	Chamonix, France
1928	Amsterdam	St. Moritz, Switzerland
1932	Los Angeles	Lake Placid, New York
1936	Berlin	Garmisch—Partenkirchen
1940	World War II	
1944	World War II	
1948	London	St. Moritz
1952	Helsinki	Oslo, Norway
1956	Melbourne	Cortina, Italy
1960	Rome	Squaw Valley, California
1964	Tokyo	Innsbruck, Austria
1968	Mexico City	Grenoble, France
1972	Munich	Sapporo, Japan
1976	Montreal	Innsbruck, Austria
1980	Moscow	Lake Placid, New York
1984	Los Angeles	Sarajevo
1988	Seoul	Alberta, Canada
1992	Barcelona	Albertville, France

159. Major World Philosophers

Peter Abelard	(1079-1142)	French
Anaxagoras	(c. 500-428 B.C.)	Greek
St. Anselm	(1033-1109)	Italian
St. Thomas Aquinas	(1225-1274)	Italian
Aristotle	(384-322 B.C.)	Greek
St. Augustine of Hippo	(354-430)	Roman
Sir Frances Bacon	(1561-1626)	English
Jeremy Bentham	(1748-1832)	English
George Berkeley	(1685-1753)	English
Martin Buber	(1878-1965)	German
Auguste Comte	(1798-1857)	French
Democratus	(c. 460-c. 370 B.C.)	Greek
René Descartes	(1596-1650)	French
John Dewey	(1859-1952)	American
Denis Diderot	(1713-1784)	French
Diogenes	(c. 400-325 B.C.)	Greek
Empedocles	(c. 495-435 B.C.)	Greek
Friedrich Engles	(1820-1895)	German
Epictetus	(c. 50-c. 138)	Greek
Epicurus	(341-270 B.C.)	Greek
Georg Wilhelm Hegel	(1770-1831)	German
Martin Heidegger	(1889-1976)	German
Thomas Hobbes	(1588-1679)	English
David Hume	(1711-1776)	English
Edmund Husserl	(1859-1938)	German
William James	(1842-1910)	American
Immanuel Kant	(1724-1804)	German
Søren Kierkegaard	(1813-1855)	Danish
Gottfried Wilhelm Leibniz	(1646-1716)	German
John Locke	(1632-1704)	English
Niccolò Machiavelli	(1469-1527)	Italian
Maimonides	(1135-1204)	Spanish
Marcus Aurelius	(121-180)	Roman
Karl Marx	(1818-1883)	German
John Stuart Mill	(1806-1873)	English
Moore, George E.	(1873-1958)	English
Sir Thomas More	(1478-1535)	English
Friedrich Wilhelm Nietzche	(1844-1900)	German
Blaise Pascal	(1623-1662)	French
Plato	(c. 428-c. 348 B.C.)	Greek
Pythagoras	(c. 582-c. 507 B.C.)	Greek
Jean Jacques Rousseau	(1712-1778)	Swiss/French
Bertrand Russell	(1872-1970)	English
George Santayana	(1863-1952)	Spanish/American
Jean-Paul Sartre	(1905-1980)	French
Arthur Schopenhauer	(1788-1860)	German

159. Major World Philosophers, continued

Adam Smith	(1723-1790)	Scottish
Socrates	(464-399 B.C.)	Greek
Benedict Spinoza	(1623-1677)	Dutch
Miguel de Unamuno	(1864-1936)	Spanish
Voltaire	(1694-1778)	French
Alfred North Whitehead	(1889-1951)	English
Zeno the Stoic	(c. 334-c. 262 B.C.)	Greek

160. Major Allies of the Persian Gulf War

Bangladesh
Britain
Egypt
France
Kuwait
Morocco
Oman
Pakistan
Qatar
Saudi Arabia
Syria
United Arab Emirates
United States

161. Continuing Wars in 1991

Afghanistan
Angola
Burma
Cambodia
Columbia
El Salvador
Ethiopia
Guatemala
India
Liberia
Mozambique
Peru
Philippines
Sahara
Somalia
Sri Lanka
Sudan

Section III

LISTS FOR AMERICAN GOVERNMENT

162. Forms of Government

Aristocracy—government ruled by the wealthy or upper class.

Autocracy—rule by one person who has total control over all others; dictatorship.

Centralism—governmental structure in which administration and power are concentrated in a central institution or group.

Constitutional monarchy—government in which the powers of the monarch are limited by and defined by a constitution.

Democracy—government in which political power is retained by all the people. In a representative democracy power may be delegated to their elected representatives.

Despotism—autocratic rule; the ruler maintins absolute power. Government in which the dictator or tyrant may possess oppressive power.

Dictatorship—government in which a ruler possesses absolute power.

Fascism—one-party system of government with individual subjected to the control of the state often by secret police, military police, censorship and government control of finance, industry, and commerce.

Federalism—union of several states under a central government, with individual states retaining specific powers under the central government.

Feudalism—a Medieval system in which vassals received land holdings in exchange for military or other service and homage to their lords.

Matriarchy—society ruled by a woman, with descent and succession being traced through the female's line.

Monarchy—sovereign control of a government by a hereditary ruler, such as a king or queen.

Oligarchy—rule of the government by a few persons.

Patriarchy—rule of a group by the father or male heir.

Republicanism—a representative democracy. Elected officials exercise power vested in them by sovereign citizens.

Theocracy—government in which the clergy rules or in which a god is the civil ruler.

Totalitarianism—system in which a highly centralized government is controlled exclusively by one party and maintained by political suppression. Other political parties are not tolerated or recognized.

163. The Cabinet Positions

Secretary of State
Secretary of the Treasury
Secretary of Defense
Attorney General
Secretary of Agriculture
Secretary of the Interior
Secretary of Housing and Urban
  Development

Secretary of Commerce
Secretary of Labor
Secretary of Transportation
Secretary of Health and Human Services
Secretary of Education
Secretary of Energy
Secretary of Veterans Affairs

164. The Bill of Rights

First Amendment. Forbids the Congress from interfering with freedom of religion, speech or press, or with the right to assemble peaceably, or to petition the government.

Second Amendment. Guarantees the right to bear arms.

Third Amendment. Assures that soldiers can not be arbitrarily lodged in private homes without the consent of the owner.

Fourth Amendment. Forbids unreasonable search or seizure of persons, homes, and effects without a warrant.

Fifth Amendment. Guarantees specific rights when on trial, including no condemnation without trial, no compulsion to be a witness against oneself, and no property taken for public use except with just compensation.

Sixth Amendment. Assures the accused right to a speedy and public trial, right to be represented by an attorney, and right to be faced by accusing witnesses.

Seventh Amendment. In lawsuits of more than $20, a trial by jury may be requested.

Eighth Amendment. Forbids excessive fines and cruel or unusual punishments.

Ninth Amendment. Just because a right is not mentioned in the Constitution does not mean that the people are not entitled to it.

Tenth Amendment. Powers not delegated to the Federal Government are

OUR RIGHTS AND OUR LIBERTIES.

165. Constitutional Amendments

Amendment XI	(1795)	prohibited citizens of one state from suing the government of another state
Amendment XII	(1804)	established separate ballots for president and vice president in electoral college
Amendment XIII	(1865)	abolished slavery
Amendment XIV	(1868)	made slaves citizens and forebade states from denying civil rights
Amendment XV	(1870)	prohibited states from dening a person the right to vote on account of race
Amendment XVI	(1913)	gave Congress the right to levy an income tax
Amendment XVII	(1913)	provided for direct election of Senators
Amendment XVIII	(1919)	permitted Congress to ban the sale of liquor
Amendment XIX	(1920)	gave women the right to vote
Amendment XX	(1933)	changed the date of the presidential inauguration and set congressional sessions to begin in January
Amendment XXI	(1933)	repealed the 18th amendment
Amendment XXII	(1951)	limited president to two elected terms
Amendment XXIII	(1961)	granted people of the District of Columbia the right to vote for presidential electors
Amendment XXIV	(1964)	prohibited use of the poll tax to deny people voting priviledges
Amendment XXV	(1967)	provided a procedure to fill the vice-presidency in the event of a vacancy
Amendment XXVI	(1971)	lowered the voting age nationally to 18

166. Expansion of the United States

Area	How obtained	Year
Louisiana	purchased from France	1803
Florida	purchased from Spain	1819
Texas	annexed	1845
Oregon	treaty with Great Britain	1846
Southwestern states	treaty with Mexico	1848
Southern Arizona	bought from Mexico	1853
Alaska	bought from Russia	1867
Hawaii	annexed	1898
Guam	treaty with Spain	1899
Puerto Rico	treaty with Spain	1899
American Samoa	treaty	1900
Virgin Islands	bought from Denmark	1917

167. States in Order of Admission to the Union

1.	Delaware	1787	26.	Michigan	1837
2.	Pennsylvania	1787	27.	Florida	1845
3.	New Jersey	1787	28.	Texas	1845
4.	Georgia	1788	29.	Iowa	1846
5.	Connecticut	1788	30.	Wisconsin	1848
6.	Massachusetts	1788	31.	California	1850
7.	Maryland	1788	32.	Minnesota	1858
8.	South Carolina	1788	33.	Oregon	1859
9.	New Hampshire	1788	34.	Kansas	1861
10.	Virginia	1788	35.	West Virginia	1863
11.	New York	1788	36.	Nevada	1864
12.	North Carolina	1789	37.	Nebraska	1867
13.	Rhode Island	1790	38.	Colorado	1876
14.	Vermont	1791	39.	North Dakota	1889
15.	Kentucky	1792	40.	South Dakota	1889
16.	Tennessee	1796	41.	Montana	1889
17.	Ohio	1803	42.	Washington	1889
18.	Louisiana	1812	43.	Idaho	1890
19.	Indiana	1816	44.	Wyoming	1890
20.	Mississippi	1817	45	Utah	1896
21.	Illinois	1818	46.	Oklahoma	1907
22.	Alabama	1819	47.	New Mexico	1912
23.	Maine	1820	48.	Arizona	1912
24.	Missouri	1821	49.	Alaska	1959
25.	Arkansas	1836	50.	Hawaii	1959

168. Federal Legal Holidays

New Year's Day	January 1
Martin Luther King Day	Third Monday in January
Washington's Birthday	Third Monday in February
Memorial Day	Last Monday in May
Independence Day	July 4
Labor Day	First Monday in September
Columbus Day	First Monday in October
Veterans' Day	November 11
Thanksgiving	Fourth Thursday in November
Christmas Day	December 25

169. Portraits on U.S. Currency

Denomination	Portrait
$1	Washington
$2	Jefferson
$5	Lincoln
$10	Hamilton
$20	Jackson
$50	Grant
$100	Franklin
$500	McKinley
$1,000	Cleveland
$5,000	Madison
$10,000	Chase
$100,000	Wilson

Bills larger than $100 are no longer issued and are removed from circulation as they are turned into the Federal Reserve.

170. Order of Succession to the President

Vice President
Speaker of the House of Representatives
President Pro Tempore of the Senate
Secretary of State
Secretary of Treasury
Secretary of Defense
Attorney General
Secretary of Interior
Secretary of Agriculture
Secretary of Commerce
Secretary of Labor
Secretary of Health and Human Services
Secretary of Housing and Urban Development
Secretary of Transportation
Secretary of Energy
Secretary of Education

171. United States Supreme Court Chief Justices

Chief Justice	Dates
John Jay	1790-1795
John Rutledge	1795*
Oliver Ellsworth	1796-1800
John Marshall	1801-1835
Roger Taney	1836-1864
Salmon P. Chase	1864-1873
Morrison R. Waite	1874-1888
Melville W. Fuller	1888-1910
Edward White	1910-1921
William H. Taft	1921-1930
Charles E. Hughes	1930-1941
Harlan Stone	1941-1946
Frederick Vinson	1946-1953
Earl Warren	1953-1969
Warren Burger	1969-1986
William Rehnquist	1986-

*Was rejected on December 15, 1795.

172. Landmark Supreme Court Personal Rights Cases

Dred Scott vs. Sandford, 1952 — Blacks are not citizens, Congress cannot ban slavery

Plessy vs. Ferguson, 1896 — Allowed "separate but equal" segregation policies

Korematsu vs. United States, 1941 — Allowed internment of U.S. Japanese during World War II

Brown vs. Topeka Board of Education, 1954 — "Separate but equal" educational facilities are unconstitutional

Engel vs. Vitale, 1962 — School prayers may not be required

Gideon vs. Wainwright, 1963 — Right to paid defense lawyer

Miranda vs. Arizona, 1966 — Accused must be informed of rights, including right to remain silent

Alexander vs. Holmes Co. Board of Ed., 1969 — Demanded immediate desegregation of all public schools

Roe vs. Wade, 1973 — States may not prevent women (under specified conditions) from having an abortion during first 6 months of pregnancy

United Steelworkers of America vs. Weber, 1979 — Affirmative action hiring programs are permitted

173. Federal Reserve Banks

District	Bank
First	Boston
Second	New York
Third	Philadelphia
Fourth	Cleveland
Fifth	Richmond
Sixth	Atlanta
Seventh	Chicago
Eighth	St. Louis
Ninth	Minneapolis
Tenth	Kansas City, MO
Eleventh	Dallas
Twelfth	San Francisco

174. Standing Congressional Committees

House of Representatives
Agriculture
Appropriations
Armed Services
Banking, Finance, and Urban
  Affairs
Budget
District of Columbia
Education and Labor
Foreign Affairs
Government Operations
House Administration
Interior and Insular Affairs
Interstate and Foreign Commerce
Judiciary
Merchant Marine and Fisheries
Post Office and Civil Service
Public Works and Transportation
Rules
Science and Technology
Small Business
Standards of Official Conduct
Veterans' Affairs
Ways and Means

Senate
Agriculture, Nutrition, and Forestry
Appropriations
Armed Services
Banking, Finance, and Urban Affairs

Budget
Commerce, Science, and Transportation
Energy and Natural Resources
Environment and Public Works
Finance
Foreign Relations
Governmental Affairs
Judiciary
Labor and Human Resources
Rules and Administration
Veterans' Affairs

175. Social Security Programs

Retirement payments
Disability payments
Survivors' payments
Medicare
Unemployment benefits
Workers' compensation

176. Kinds of Taxes

capital gains
excess profits
excise
franchise
gasoline
income
inheritance
license
poll
property
sales
tariff
value-added

177. Military Ranks: Officers

Army, Marine, Air Force	Navy
General	Fleet Admiral
Lieutenant General	Admiral
Major General	Vice Admiral
Brigadier General	Rear Admiral
Colonel	Commodore
Lieutenant Colonel	Captain
Major	Commander
Captain	Lieutenant Commander
First Lieutenant	Lieutenant
Second Lieutenant	Lieutenant Junior Grade
Chief Warrant Officer	Ensign
Warrant Officer	Chief Warrant Officer
	Warrant Officer

178. Presidents of the United States

President	Served	President	Served
George Washington	1789-1797	Chester A. Arthur	1881-1885
John Adams	1797-1801	Grover Cleveland	1885-1889
Thomas Jefferson	1801-1809	Benjamin Harrison	1889-1893
James Madison	1809-1817	Grover Cleveland	1893-1897
James Monroe	1817-1825	William McKinley	1897-1901
John Quincy Adams	1825-1829	Theodore Roosevelt	1901-1909
Andrew Jackson	1829-1837	William H. Taft	1909-1913
Martin Van Buren	1837-1841	Woodrow Wilson	1913-1921
William Henry Harrison	1841-1841	Warren G. Harding	1921-1923
John Tyler	1841-1845	Calvin Coolidge	1925-1929
James K. Polk	1845-1849	Herbert Hoover	1929-1933
Zachary Taylor	1849-1850	Franklin D. Roosevelt	1933-1945
Millard Fillmore	1850-1853	Harry S. Truman	1945-1953
Franklin Pierce	1853-1857	Dwight D. Eisenhower	1953-1961
James Buchanan	1857-1861	John F. Kennedy	1961-1963
Abraham Lincoln	1861-1865	Lyndon B. Johnson	1963-1969
Andrew Johnson	1865-1869	Richard M. Nixon	1969-1974
Ulysses S. Grant	1869-1877	Gerald R. Ford	1974-1977
Rutherford B. Hayes	1877-1881	James E. Carter, Jr.	1977-1981
James A. Garfield	1881-1881	Ronald Reagan	1981-1989
		George Bush	1989-

179. Presidents Who Were Not Lawyers

President	Occupation
George Washington	planter, solider
William Henry Harrison	soldier, farmer
Zachary Taylor	soldier
Andrew Johnson	tailor
Ulyssess S. Grant	soldier
Theodore Roosevelt	author, public official
Woodrow Wilson	educator
Warren G. Harding	newspaper editor
Herbert Hoover	engineer
Harry S. Truman	businessman
Dwight D. Eisenhower	soldier
John F. Kennedy	author, public official
Lyndon B. Johnson	teacher, public official
James E. Carter, Jr.	businessman
Ronald Reagan	actor

180. Vice Presidents of the United States

John Adams*	1789-1797	Thomas Hendricks	1885
Thomas Jefferson*	1797-1801	Levi Morton	1889-1893
Aaron Burr	1801-1805	Adlai E. Stevenson	1893-1897
George Clinton	1805-1812	Garrett Hobart	1897-1899
Elbrige Gerry	1813-1814	Theodore Roosevelt*	1901
Daniel Tompkins	1817-1825	Charles Fairbanks	1905-1909
John C. Calhoun	1825-1832	James Sherman	1909-1912
Martin Van Buren*	1833-1837	Calvin Coolidge*	1921-1923
Richard Johnson	1837-1841	Charles Dawes	1925-1929
John Tyler*	1841	Charles Curtis	1929-1933
George Dallas	1845-1849	John N. Garner	1933-1941
Millard Fillmore*	1849-1850	Henry Wallace	1941-1945
William King	1853	Harry S. Truman*	1945
John C. Breckinridge	1857-1861	Alben Barkley	1949-1953
Hannibal Hamlin	1861-1865	Richard Nixon*	1953-1961
Andrew Johnson*	1865	Lyndon B. Johnson*	1961-1963
Schuyler Colfax	1869-1873	Hubert Humphrey	1965-1969
Henry Wilson	1873-1875	Spiro Agnew	1969-1973
William Wheeler	1877-1881	Gerald Ford*	1973-1974
Chester A. Arthur*	1881	Nelson Rockefeller	1974-1977
		Walter Mondale	1977-1981
		George Bush*	1981-1989
		Dan Quayle	1989-

*later served as president

181. Federalist Candidates for President

1788	George Washington
1792	George Washington
1796	John Adams
1800	John Adams
1804	Charles Pinckney
1808	Charles Pinckney
1812	DeWitt Clinton
1816	Rufus King

182. Whig Candidates for President

1832	Henry Clay
1836	William H. Harrison
1840	William H. Harrison
1844	Henry Clay
1848	Zackary Taylor
1852	Winfield Scott
1856	Millard Fillmore

183. Republican Candidates for President

1856	John C. Frémont
1860	Abraham Lincoln
1864	Abraham Lincoln
1868	Ulysses S. Grant
1872	Ulysses S. Grant
1876	Rutherford B. Hayes
1880	James Garfield
1884	James G. Blaine
1888	Benjamin Harrison
1892	Benjamin Harrison
1896	William McKinley
1900	William McKinley
1904	Theodore Roosevelt
1908	William H. Taft
1912	William H. Taft
1916	Charles E. Hughes
1920	Warren G. Harding
1924	Calvin Coolidge
1928	Herbert Hoover
1932	Herbert Hoover
1936	Alf Landon
1940	Wendell Wilkie
1944	Thomas Dewey
1948	Thomas Dewey
1952	Dwight D. Eisenhower
1956	Dwight D. Eisenhower
1960	Richard Nixon
1964	Barry Goldwater
1968	Richard Nixon
1972	Richard Nixon
1976	Gerald Ford
1980	Ronald Reagan
1984	Ronald Reagan
1988	George Bush

184. Democratic Candidates for President

1796	Thomas Jefferson*	1896	William J. Bryan
1800	Thomas Jefferson*	1900	William J. Bryan
1804	Thomas Jefferson*	1904	Alton B. Parker
1808	James Madison*	1908	William J. Bryan
1812	James Madison*	1912	Woodrow Wilson
1816	James Monroe*	1916	Woodrow Wilson
1820	James Monroe*	1920	James Cox
1824	John Quincy Adams*	1924	John W. Davis
1828	Andrew Jackson	1928	Alfred E. Smith
1832	Andrew Jackson	1932	Franklin D. Roosevelt
1836	Martin Van Buren	1936	Franklin D. Roosevelt
1840	Martin Van Buren	1940	Franklin D. Roosevelt
1844	James K. Polk	1944	Franklin D. Roosevelt
1848	Lewis Cass	1948	Harry Truman
1852	Franklin Pierce	1952	Adlai E. Stevenson
1856	James Buchanan	1956	Adlai E. Stevenson
1860	Stephen Douglas	1960	John F. Kennedy
1864	George McClellan	1964	Lyndon B. Johnson
1868	Horatio Seymour	1968	Hubert H. Humphrey
1872	Horace Greeley	1972	George McGovern
1876	Samuel Tilden	1976	James E. Carter, Jr.
1880	Winfield Hancock	1980	James E. Carter, Jr.
1884	Grover Cleveland	1984	Walter Mondale
1888	Grover Cleveland	1988	Michael Dukakis
1892	Grover Cleveland		

*Includes the Democratic-Republicans, predecessors to the Democratic Party

185. Debate Topics

The military draft should be reinstated.

Compulsory education should be abolished.

Corporal punishment should be banned from all schools.

The electoral college should be abolished.

Affirmative action programs are no longer needed.

Communism is dead.

All students should be required to learn a foreign language.

The presidential term should be lengthened to six years.

Representatives and senators should have a limited number of terms.

The health care system should be socialized to guarantee medical care to all.

A national competency examination for high school graduation should be enacted.

Foreign ownership of American property should be restricted.

The presidential primary election should be abolished.

Television advertising for beer should be banned.

Puerto Rico should be granted statehood.

The death penalty should be abolished.

The world is a better place to live today than 100 years ago.

Democracy is the best form of government for all peoples of the world.

The U.S. Government must finance a national high speed rail system.

The United States must maintain a role as the "world's policeman."

All advertisements for cigarettes should be prohibited.

The inheritance tax should be abolished.

All students are entitled to a college educaton, even if they can not afford to pay for it themselves.

Gambling should be legalized.

The use of all mind-altering drugs should be legalized.

Mandatory drug testing on the job should not be permitted.

The motto "In God we trust" should be removed form U.S. money.

Local schools should be free to determine whether or not to teach the theory of evolution.

The U.S. Government must finance the search for an alternative fuel to oil.

Women should be used in combat roles.

186. Significant Third Parties

Party	Election
Anti-Masonic	1832
Free-Soil	1848
American ("Know Nothing")	1856
Southern Democrats	1860
Constitutional Union	1860
Populist	1892
Socialist	1912
Progressive ("Bull Moose")	1912
Progressive	1924
American Independent	1968
Independent	1980

187. Presidents with Most Vetoes

F. D. Roosevelt	635
Cleveland	584
Truman	258
Eisenhower	188
Grant	93
T. Roosevelt	82

188. Presidents Who Died in Office

William H. Harrison, 1841
Zackary Taylor, 1850
Abraham Lincoln, 1865*
James Garfield, 1881*
William McKinley*
Warren G. Harding
Franklin D. Roosevelt
John F. Kennedy*

*assassinated

189. Presidential Firsts

First President . . .	President
to accept no salary as President	George Washington
to appear on a U.S. postage stamp	George Washington
to reside in Washington, D.C.	John Adams
whose son became President	John Adams
to be inaugurated in Washington, D.C.	Thomas Jefferson
to be a widower when elected	Thomas Jefferson
to have been a Congressman	James Madison
to be a Senator	James Monroe
to have a billiard table in the White House	John Q. Adams
Phi Beta Kappa member	John Q. Adams
born in a log cabin	Andrew Jackson
to ride on a railroad	Andrew Jackson
to pay off the national debt	Andrew Jackson
to marry a divorceé	Andrew Jackson
to receive an assassination attempt	Andrew Jackson
nominated at a national convention	Andrew Jackson
to have fought a duel	Andrew Jackson
born a citizen of the United States	Martin Van Buren
to die in office	William H. Harrison
married during his term in office	John Tyler
to be burned in effigy on the White House lawn	John Tyler
to have served as Speaker of the House	James K. Polk
to install a bathtub in the White House	Millard Fillmore
to be a bachelor	James Buchanan
assassinated	Abraham Lincoln
to wear a beard	Abraham Lincoln
depicted on a U.S. coin	Abraham Lincoln
to receive a patent	Abraham Lincoln
to have served as a preacher	Andrew Johnson
to be a graduate of West Point	Ulyssess S. Grant
to use a telephone	James Garfield
who was also a preacher	James Garfield
whose mother saw him inaugurated	James Garfield
married in the White House	Grover Cleveland
to ride in an automobile	Theodore Roosevelt
to receive a Nobel Peace prize	Theodore Roosevelt
to fly in an airplane	Theodore Roosevelt
to ride in a submarine	Theodore Roosevelt
to become chief justice of the Supreme Court	William Howard Taft
buried in Arlington National Cemetery	William Howard Taft
to throw out a baseball to open the season	Wiliiam Howard Taft
to visit Europe while in office	Woodrow Wilson

189. Presidential Firsts, continued

First President . . .	President
to earn a doctorate	Woodrow Wilson
to use loud speakers at his inauguration	Warren G. Harding
to speak over radio	Warren G. Harding
to ride an auto at his inaugural	Warren G. Harding
see talking pictures in the White House	Calvin Coolidge
born west of the Mississippi	Herbert Hoover
to have a phone on his desk	Herbert Hoover
to be a millionaire	Herbert Hoover
inaugurated on January 20	Franklin D. Roosevelt
to fly in an airplane while in office	Franklin D. Roosevelt
to have air conditioning in the White House	Franklin D. Roosevelt
to be elected more than two terms	Franklin D. Roosevelt
to ride a diesel train	Franklin D. Roosevelt
to appear on television	Franklin D. Roosevelt
to fly in a helicopter	Dwight D. Eisenhower
to earn an airplane pilot's license	Dwight D. Eisenhower
to appear on color television	Dwight D. Eisenhower
who was a Catholic	John F. Kennedy
to appoint his brother to the cabinet	John F. Kennedy
to resign from office	Richard Nixon
whose parents were divorced	Gerald Ford
born in a hospital	Jimmy Carter
to have been divorced	Ronald Reagan

190. Historic Sites in Washington, D.C.

Arlington National Cemetery
Blair House
Ford's Theatre
Government Printing Office
J. Edgar Hoover Building (FBI)
Jefferson Memorial
Library of Congress
Lincoln Memorial
National Archives
Pentagon
Smithsonian Museums
Supreme Court Building
Tomb of the Unknown Soldier
United States Capitol Building
Vietnam Memorial
Washington Monument
Watergate Hotel
White House

191. Civil Rights Organizations

American Arab Anti-Discrimination Committee, 1980
American Civil Liberties Union, 1895
Americans for Democratic Action, 1947
Anti-Defamation League of B'nai B'rith, 1913
Congress of Racial Equality, 1942
National Association for the Advancement of Colored People, 1909
National Urban League, 1919
Operation PUSH (People United to Save Humanity). 1976
Southern Christian Leadership Conference, 1957
Student Non-violent Coordinating Committee, 1960

192. Early Black Civil Rights Leaders

Richard Allen	1760-1831
Mary Jane Bethune	1875-1955
Frederick Douglas	1817-1895
W.E.B. DuBois	1868-1963
Henry H. Garnet	1815-1882
Marcus Garvey	1887-1940
Lester Granger	1896-1976
Eugene Jones	1884-1951
Martin Luther King, Jr.	1929-1968
Malcolm X	1925-1965
Kelly Miller	1863-1939
Mary Church Terrell	1863-1954
Harriet Ross Tubman	1820-1913
Roy Wilkins	1910-1981
Whitney Young, Jr.	1922-1971

193. Miranda Rights

You have the right to remain silent and not answer any questions.

If you choose to speak, anything you say may be used in a court of law against you.

You have the right to talk with a lawyer before talking to the police and to have a lawyer present when you are talking to the police.

If you do not have a lawyer, you have the right to remain silent until you have contacted one.

If you cannot afford a lawyer, the court will appoint one for you.

194. Current Supreme Court Members

(In order of seniority)
Byron R. White
Thurgood Marshall
Harry A. Blackmun
William H. Rehnquist (chief justice)
John Paul Stevens III
Sandra Day O'Connor
Antonin Scalia
Anthony M. Kennedy
David H. Souter

195. Journals Related to Government

Administration and Society
American Journal of Political
 Science
American Politics Quarterly
American Spectator, The
Bureaucrat, The
Columbia Journal of Law and
 Social Problems
Comparative Political Studies
Congressional Quarterly
Contemporary Policy Issues
Critical Review
Employee Relations Law Journal
Global Affairs
Harvard Law Review
Human Rights Quarterly
International Journal of Public
 Administration
Journal of Church and State
Journal of Conflict Resolution
Journal of International Affairs
Journal of Law and Society
Journal of Political and Military
 Sociology
Journal of Public Policy
Law and Policy
Law and Social Inquiry
Law and Society Review
Legislative Studies Quarterly
New Left Review

New Statesman and Society
Northwest University Law Review
Peace and Change
Philosophy and Public Affairs
Policy Sciences
Policy Studies Journal
Political Science Quarterly
Political Studies
Political Theory
Politics
Popular Government
Population Bulletin
Presidential Studies Quarterly
Public Administration
Public Administration Quarterly
Public Administration Review
Public Choice
Publius: The Journal of
 Federalism
Reason
Society
Southern California Law Review
Texas Law Review
Theory and Decision
Vietnam Generation
Western Political Quarterly
Without Prejudice
World Policy Journal

Section IV

LISTS FOR CONSUMER ECONOMICS

196. Primary Federal Consumer Protection Agencies

Consumer Product Safety Commission
Environmental Protection Agency
Federal Reserve System
Federal Trade Commission
Food and Drug Administration
Food Safety and Quality Service
National Highway Safety Administration
United States Postal Inspection Service
United States Attorney General's Office

197. Areas Needing Consumer Protection

false or misleading advertising
excessive interest rates
pollution of the environment
against the power of monopolies
unfair selling practices
selling harmful products
deceptive labeling

198. How to Complain Effectively

Save and submit any receipts or warranties
Get your facts first
Allow a reasonable time for action
Be specific about what you want
Avoid personal attacks; use objective language
Contact the Better Business Bureau for advice on options
Learn how to use the small claims court
Check out relevant trade associations
Be persistent

199. Life Expectancy of New Appliances

Appliance	Average Years of Use
Electric Sewing Machine	24
Electric Range	16
Gas Range	16
Electric Refrigerator	16
Tank Vacuum Cleaner	15
Electric Toaster	15
Electric Clothes Dryer	14
Television Set	11
Automatic Washer	10

Source: Consumer and Food Economics Research Division, U.S. Department of Agriculture.

200. Metric Conversion

Length U.S. unit	Metric equivalent	Length Metric	U.S. equivalent
inch	2.54 centimeters	millimeter	.039 inches
foot	30.48 centimeters	centimeter	.394 inches
yard	.914 meters	decimeter	3.937 inches
rod	5.029 meters	meter	39.37 inches
mile	1.609	kilometer	.621 mile

Capacity		Capacity	
pint	.473 liters	milliliter	0.34 fluid ounces
quart	.946 liters	1 liter	1.057 liquid quarts
gallon	3.79 liters	1 kililiter	264.18 gallons

201. Liquid Measures

4 gills = 1 pint
2 pints = 1 quart
4 quarts = 1 gallon
31½ gallons = 1 barrel
2 barrels = 1 hogshead

202. Length Measurements

12 inches = 1 foot
3 feet = 1 yard
5½ yards = 1 rod or pole
40 rods = 1 furlong
8 furlongs = 1 statute mile (5,280 feet)

203. Nautical Measurements

6 feet = 1 fathom
120 fathoms = 1 cable length
6082 feet = 1 nautical mile

204. Area Measurements

144 sq. inches = 1 sq. foot
9 sq. feet = 1 sq. yard
30¼ sq. yards = 1 sq. rod
160 sq. rods = 1 acre
640 sq. rods = 1 sq. mile
6 sq. miles = 1 township

205. Household Measures

Unit	Equivalent
teaspoon	⅙ fluid ounce
tablespoon	3 teaspoons
cup	16 tablespoons
pint	2 cups
quart	2 pints
gallon	4 quarts
peck	8 quarts
bushel	4 pecks

206. Weight Measures

1 carat = 200 milligrams = 3.086 grains
1 gram = .001 kilograms = .035 ounces
1 milligram = .001 grams
1 ounce = 28 grams
1 pound = 16 ounces = 453.6 grams
1 kilogram = 1,000 grams = 2.21 pounds
1 short ton = 2,000 pounds
1 long ton = 2,240 pounds

207. Dry Measures

2 pints = 1 quart
8 quarts = 1 peck
4 pecks = 1 bushel
3.28 bushels = 1 barrel

208. Hottest Job Prospects in the Next Decade

cashiers
computer programmers
computer systems analysts
data processing equipment repairers
dental hygenists
employment interviewers
food counter workers
general managers
general office clerks
guards
home health aides
janitors, maids
medical assistants
medical records technicians
nursing aides, orderlies
occupational therapists
optometrists
paralegals
physical therapists
physical therapy aides
podiatrists
radiologic technologists & technicians
registered nurses
sales clerks
surgical technicians
top executives
truck drivers
waiters & waitresses

Source: U.S. Dept. of Labor

209. Career Opportunities in Economics

account executive
bank manager
claims adjuster
consumer advocate
credit manager
economic development planner
economic forecaster
econometrician
economist
environmental economist
financial analyst
fund raiser
internal auditor
investment counselor
labor specialist
loan counselor
lobbyist
market researcher
marketing representative
microeconomist
mortgage loan officer
portfolio administrator
rate analyst
real estate broker
rent control administrator
revenue officer
risk analyst
securities analyst
stock broker
tax auditor
teacher
underwriter
urban planner

210. Investment Opportunities

art and collectibles
bonds
certificates of deposit
common stocks
preferred stocks
GNMA's
gold and precious metals
limited partnerships
money market accounts
municipal bonds
mutual funds, bond
mutual funds, stock
NOW accounts
passbook savings accounts
real estate
unit trusts
U.S. notes and bonds
U.S. savings bonds
U.S. treasury bills
zero coupon bonds

211. Types of Mortgages

adjustable rate mortgage
assumable mortgage
balloon mortgage
fixed rate mortgage
graduated payment mortgage
graduated payment adjustable rate mortgage
growing equity mortgage
home equity mortgage
installment contract
interest rate buydowns
lease with option to buy
seller mortgage
shared appreciation mortgage
shared equity mortgage
wrap-around mortgage
zero interest mortgage

212. Best Time to Buy

January
- appliances
- books
- carpeting
- china
- furniture
- furs
- houses
- linen, white goods
- shoes
- tools
- towels

February
- housewares
- electronic appliances
- men's clothing
- sports equipment
- toys
- used cars

March
- children's shoes
- garden supplies
- ice skates
- luggage
- ski equipment

April
- paint supplies
- women's shoes

May
- lawn furniture
- purses
- shoes

June
- women's shoes

July
- appliances
- luggage
- summer clothes
- summer sports gear
- swimming suits

August
- coats
- furniture
- linen, white goods
- school clothes
- tires

September
- cars
- bicycles
- fall clothing
- gardening supplies

October
- cars
- china
- coats
- school supplies
- winter clothing

November
- blankets
- large appliances
- men's suits
- shoes

December
- after Christmas sales
- hats
- houses
- used cars

213. Personal Budget Expenses

rent or mortgage payments
property taxes
electricity, gas, oil
water & sewer
maintenance
property insurance
telephone
car payments
auto insurance
maintenance & repairs
taxes, auto tags, fees
parking
gas & oil
groceries
meals away from home
clothing
laundry, dry cleaning

doctors, dentists
medical supplies
health insurance
life insurance
personal care
education
vacations
recreation, movies
subsciptions & books
hobbies
dues to clubs and organizations
church donations
donations to charities
gifts
savings
interest on credit cards
misc. expenses

214. Parts of a Check

account number
American Bankers Association routing number
amount in numbers
amount in words
check issue date
check number
check writer's signature
memo
payee
pay
routing information
writer's name and address
endorsement line (on back)

215. Sources of Loans

state or federal guaranteed student loans
personal loans from banks
pawnshops
friends, relatives
against cash value of insurance
bank charge cards
savings and loan institutions
banks
credit unions
co-signed loans from banks
second mortgage bank loans
seller financed mortgages
unsecured personal loans

216. Personal Assets

equity in home
automobile
retirement fund
household items, furniture
savings account
checking account
stocks
bonds
mutual funds
other investments, collections
insurance cash value
money owed to you
cash

217. Ways to Improve Gas Mileage

steady acceleration, avoid jack rabbit starts
minimize short trips, combine shorter errands
change oil and filters as specified by auto manufacturer
keep carburetor and ignition system tuned
slow down, mileage decreases above 55 mph
avoid heavy loads when possible
rough roads will decrease mileage
use air conditioning only when necessary
driving into headwinds cuts fuel economy
cold weather will yield lower mileage

218. Household Safety Checklist

storage rack for knives
ladders properly maintained
secure handrails on all stairs
know how to turn off gas main
night lights used
medicines out of reach of children
non-skid mat in shower or tub
no electric appliances near sink
proper stair treads
appliances properly grounded
door off any unused refrigerator
emergency numbers readily available
proper guards on any power tools
use of goggles with power tools
power tools grounded
appropriate lighting in work areas
safety glass installed in all doors
dead limbs trimmed from trees

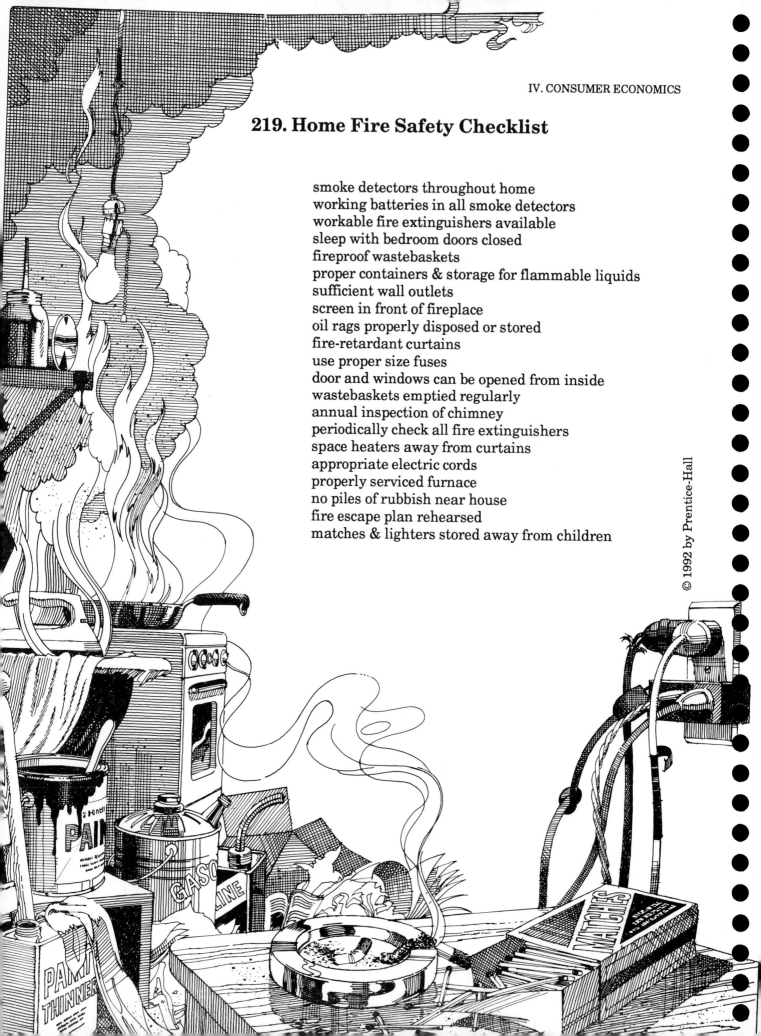

219. Home Fire Safety Checklist

smoke detectors throughout home
working batteries in all smoke detectors
workable fire extinguishers available
sleep with bedroom doors closed
fireproof wastebaskets
proper containers & storage for flammable liquids
sufficient wall outlets
screen in front of fireplace
oil rags properly disposed or stored
fire-retardant curtains
use proper size fuses
door and windows can be opened from inside
wastebaskets emptied regularly
annual inspection of chimney
periodically check all fire extinguishers
space heaters away from curtains
appropriate electric cords
properly serviced furnace
no piles of rubbish near house
fire escape plan rehearsed
matches & lighters stored away from children

220. Labor Unions

Amalgamated Clothing and Textile Workers Union (ACTWU)

American Federation of Labor & Congress of Industrial Organizations (AFL-CIO)

American Federation of Musicians of the United States and Canada (AF of M)

American Federation of State, County and Municipal Employees

Actors Equity Association

Airline Pilots Association

Allied Industrial Workers of America (AIW)

Aluminum Brick & Glass Workers International Union (ABG-WIU)

American Association of University Professors (AAUP)

American Federation of Government Employees (AFGE)

American Federation of Teachers (AFT)

American Postal Workers Union (APWU)

Bakery, Confectionary & Tobacco Workers International Union (BC&T)

Brotherhood of Railway, Airline and Steamship Clerks, Freight Handlers, Express and Station Employees (BRAC)

Brotherhood of Painters and Allied Trades (IBPAT)

Carpenters and Joiners of America

Chemical Workers Union

Communication Workers of America

Farm Workers of America (UFW)

Food and Commercial Workers International Union (UFCW)

Fraternal Order of Police

Glass, Pottery, Plastics & Allied Workers International Union (GPPAW)

Graphic Communications International Union (GCIU)

Hotel Employees and Restaurant Employees International Union

International Association of Firefighters

International Brotherhood of Electrical Workers (IBEW)

United Paperhangers International Union (UPIC) Brotherhood of Teamsters, Chauffeurs, Warehousemen and Helpers of America (IBT)

International Association of Bridge, Structural and Ornamental Iron Workers

220. Labor Unions, continued

International Ladies Garment Workers Union

International Ladies Garment Workers Union Longshoremen's Association

Laborers' International Union of North America

Machinists and Aerospace Workers

National Association of Letter Carriers (NALC)

National Education Association (NEA)

Oil Chemical, and Atomic Workers International Union (OCAW)

Retail, Wholessale and Department Store Union

Service Employees International Union (REIU)

Sheet Metal Workers' International Association (SMWIA)

Union of Operating Engineers (IUOE)

United Garment Workers of America (UGWA)

United Mines Workers of America (UMWA)

United Paperhangers International Union (UPIU)

United Steelworkers of America (USWA)

United Transportation Union (UTU)

221. Factors to Consider in Selecting a Car

braking ability
cargo room
convenience of controls
convenience of
  displays
color
comfort
cost
dealer's reputation
gas mileage (mpg)
head room
leg room
maneuverability
noise, riding
options available
power
reliability
repair record
safety rating
service availability
smoothness of ride
style
transmission, smooth shifting
trunk space
warranty

222. Factors Affecting the Cost of a Diamond

color
clarity
cut
carat weight

223. Factors to Consider in Selecting a College

admission standards
advising services
attractiveness of campus
campus safety record
climate
cost
distance from home
employment placement services
extracurriculuar activities
financial aid
majors availability
male-female ratio
number of students
reputation of faculty
student-faculty ratio
student faculty relationships
student services

224. Abbreviations of Academic Degrees

B.A.	Bachelor of Arts	D.S.	Doctor of Science
B.B.A.	Bachelor of Business Administration	D.V.M.	Doctor of Veterinary Medicine
B.D.	Bachelor of Divinity		
B.E.	Bachelor of Education	Ed.B.	Bachelor of Education
B.E.E.	Bachelor of Electrical Engineering	Ed.D.	Doctor of Education
B.F.A.	Bachelor of Fine Arts	Ed.M.	Master of Education
B.L.S.	Bachelor of Library Science	E.E.	Electrical Engineer
B.S.	Bachelor of Science	J.D.	Doctor of Jurisprudence
B.T.	Bachelor of Theology		
C.E.	Civil Engineer	L.B.	Bachelor of Letters
Ch.D.	Doctor of Chemistry	L.H.D.	Doctor of Humanities
Ch.E.	Chemical Engineer	LL.D.	Doctor of Laws
D.C.	Doctor of Chiropractic	M.A.	Master of Arts
D.D.	Doctor of Divinity	M.Agr.	Master of Agriculture
D.D.S.	Doctor of Dental Surgery	M.B.A.	Master of Business Administration
D.F.A.	Doctor of Fine Arts		
D.L.S.	Doctor of Library Science	M.D.	Doctor of Medicine
D.O.	Doctor of Osteopathy	M.S.W.	Masters of Social Work
		Ph.D.	Doctor of Philosophy
		Psy.D.	Doctor of Psychology

225. American Architectural Styles

Art Deco
Art Moderne
Bungalow
Cape Cod
Chateau
Colonial Revival
Dutch Colonial
Egyptian Revival
Georgian
Gothic Revival
Greek Revival
Federal
French Colonial
Italian Villa
Italianate
International
Mission
Octagon
Prairie
Pueblo
Queen Anne
Ranch
Renaissance Revival
Roman Classicism
Romanesque
Revival
Saltbox
Second Empire
Second Renaissance Revival
Shingle
Southern Colonial
Spanish Colonial
Split-Level
Sullivanesque
Victorian Gothic
Victorian Romanesque

226. Economics Related Journals

The Action Faction
The American Economic Review
The American Economist
American Journal of Economics
 and Sociology
Business Economics
Canadian Consumer
Challenge
Changing Times
Consumer Bulletin
Consumer Life
Consumer Reports
Consumer's Digest Magazine
Dollars and Sense
Economic Development and
 Cultural Change
Economic Facts
Economic Geography
Economic Inquiry
The Energy Journal
Explorations in Economic History
FDA Consumer
The Financial Review
Fortune
Growth and Change
Harvard Business Review
Inquiry
The Journal of Behavioral Economics
Journal of Comparative Economics
Journal of Developmental Economics
Journal of Economic Behavior and Organization

Journal of Economic Education
Journal of Economic Issues
Journal of Health Economics
Journal of Labor Research
Journal of Marketing
Journal of Political Economy
Journal of Retailing
Journal of Urban Economics
Labor History
Money
Monthly Labor Review
New England Economic Review
Problems of Communism
Public Choice
Quarterly Review of Economics and
 Business
Review of Social Economy
Southern Economic Journal

Section V

LISTS FOR SOCIOLOGY

227. Careers in Sociology

charities administrator	market researcher
child welfare advocate	mediator
clinical social worker	ministry
community organizer	population analyst
census analyst	public opinion pollster
consultant	psychiatric social worker
cottage supervisor	recreation worker
criminal justice planner	researcher
customer relations	rural sociologist
demographer	school social worker
geriatric social worker	social services volunteer coordinator
group worker	social worker
houseparent	sociology professor
industrial sociologist	substance abuse counselor
interviewer	training and development
labor relations	urban planner
law enforement officer	youth care worker

228. Pioneers in the Field of Sociology

Ruth Benedict
Jeremy Bentham
Charles H. Cooley
John Dewey
W.E.B. DuBois
Erich Fromm
Erving Goffman
William James
Lawrence Kohlberg
Elizabeth Kübler-Ross
Kurt Lewin
Konrad Lorenz
Margaret Mead
David Riesman
Max Weber

229. U.S. Social Reformers

Edith Abbott (1876-1957)
Grace Abbott (1878-1939)
Jane Addams (1860-1935)
Susan B. Anthony (1820-1906)
Gamaliel Bailey (1807-1859)
Clara Barton (1821-1912)
Henry Ward Beecher (1813-1887)
Amelia Bloomer (1818-1894)
William Booth (1829-1894)
Elihu Burritt (1811-1879)
Carrie Chapman Catt (1859-1947)
John Jay Chapman (1862-1933)
Dorothy Day (1897-1980)
Eugene Debs (1855-1926)
Dorothea Dix (1802-1887)
Fredrick Douglas (1817-1895)
W.E.B. DuBois (1868-1963)
William Lloyd Garrison (1805-1879)
Samuel G. Howe (1801-1876)
Helen Keller (1880-1968)
Robert La Follette (1855-1925)
Joshua Leavitt (1794-1873)
Martin Luther King, Jr. (1929-1968)
Horace Mann (1796-1859)
Lucretia Mott (1793-1880)
Wendell Phillips (1811-1884)
Jacob Riis (1849-1914)
Margaret Sanger (1883-1966)
Elizabeth Cady Stanton (1815-1902)
Lucy Stone (1818-1893)
Harriet Tubman (1820-1913)
Booker T. Washington (1856-1915)
Walter F. White (1893-1955)
Emma Hart Willard (1787-1870)
Frances E. Willard (1839-1898)
Whitney M. Young, Jr. (1921-1971)

230. Problems Facing Teenagers

Alcohol abuse
Drug abuse
Peer pressures
Teenage pregnancy
AIDS, venereal disease
Career uncertainties
Financing college
Getting along with parents
Getting into college
Grades
Sibling relationships
Physical safety, gangs
Family economics
Unemployment
Fear of war
Parents' divorce
School problems
Teenage suicide
Problems in growing up
Sexual identity
Drugs

231. Fields of Study in Sociology

criminology
demography
human ecology
marriage and family studies
political sociology
popular culture
social psychology
sociolinguistics
sociometry
sociology of education
sociology of law
suicidology
urban sociology

232. Folk Medicines

Ailment	Treatment
asthma	wear a muskrat skin over the lungs
bed-wetting	honey; eat fried mouse pie
bleeding	chimney soot
body odor	baking soda
boils	poultice of ginger and flour
bug bites	apply baking soda or meat
burns	apple honey
chest cold	a mustard-lard plaster placed on chest
chiggers	salty pig skin
colds	onion and honey soup
colds	rub skunk grease on the chest
consumption	tar and egg yolks
cough	mixture of honey, lemon & whiskey
croupe	turpentine in a spoonful of sugar
dandruff	vinegar water
earache prevention	wear wool from a black sheep in the ear
earache	warm vinegar water in the ear
hangover	scrambled owl's eggs
impaired vision	piercing an ear
laziness	balm tea
mosquito bites	baking soda
nose bleeds	tea leaves
onion breath	drink coffee
pimples	apply thin white skin from inside egg shell
pimples	salve made of wheat germ and milk
poison ivy	apply paste made of baking soda and water
rheumatism	wear the eye tooth of a pig
sore throat	gargle with apple cider vinegar
stuffed-up nose	chew honeycomb
sunburn	wash with sage tea
toothache	chew cotton; oil of cloves
upset stomach	boil elm broth; vinegar water; castor oil
varicose veins	apply apple cider vinegar
warts	rub with radish or raw meat
warts	tie a toad around your neck

233. Esperanto Vocabulary

Esperanto is an international language first proposed by Dr. L. L. Zamenhof in 1887. It is currently spoken by several million people in over 80 countries.

Esperanto	English	Esperanto	English
arbo	tree	tute no	not at all
bel	beautiful	patro	father
besto	animal	pren	take
bibro	book	ricevas	receive
blua	blue	skribas	writes
bona	good	tablo	table
ced	yield	tago	day
cit	quote	tre	very
diferenc	difference	tro	too
diskut	discuss	venas	come
donas	give	vi	you
dankas	thank	nulo	0
esperaas	hope	unu	1
far	do, make	du	2
fort	strong	tri	3
gust	taste	kvar	4
havas	has, have	kvin	5
instruisto	teacher	ses	6
ir	go	sep	7
jes	yes	ok	8
kredas	believe	nau	9
ne	no, not	dek	10
nigra	black	cent	100
nova	new	mil	1000

For more information contact:
Education Department
Esperanto League
P.O. Box 1129
El Cerrito, CA 94530

234. Dialects of the United States

Appalachian
Black English
Bostoniaan
Bronx
Brooklyn
Chesapeake Bay
    (Maryland & Virginia coast)
Conch (Florida Keys)
Creole (Louisiana)
General American
Gullah (South Carolina
    & Georgia coast)

Gumbo
Louisiana Cajun
Midwestern
New York City
Outer Banks (North Carolina coast)
Ozark
Pennsylvania Dutch
Southern
Upper New York State
Western drawl
Yankee (New England)
Yiddish American

235. Cowboy Slang

Slang	Meaning	Slang	Meaning
amigo	friend	nutcrackers	teeth
Arkansas toothpick	long knife	outfox	to outsmart
axlegrease	butter	pearl diver	dishwasher
bandido	outlaw	Pecos Bill	liar
bar dog	bartender	rib wrenches	spurs
bean master	cook	rildy	a blanket
belly-wash	weak coffee	roll the cotton	to break camp
bone orchard	cemetery	sage rat	someone living in the desert
buffalo chip	dried buffalo manure		
bunkhouse	cowhand's building	salty dog	someone who does a good job
burro milk	nonsense!		
caboodle	whole thing, all	shindig	a dance, fancy affair
cahoots	partnership	stood up	robbed
chuck	food	wallow in velvet	to be wealthy
dough roller	cook		
dude	visitor from East	wrangle	to herd horses
eatin' irons	knives, forks, spoons		
flea trap	bed roll		
fodder forker	farmer		
great joint	cafe, restaurant		
gully-washer	heavy rain		
high-tail	to leave suddenly		
hill rat	prospector working in the hills		
hoedown	dance		
hot rock	biscuit		
idiot stick	a shovel		
kack	saddle		
lead pusher	gun		
long trail	death		
look-see	to investigate		
necktie party	a hanging		

236. Fads and Fancies of the 80's

acid washed jeans
aerobic dancing
argyle checked socks
baggy sweaters
"Baby on Board" signs
beepers
blackened redfish
bottled war
break dancing
button fly denim jeans
Cabbage Patch dolls
call waiting
charm bracelets
ceiling fans
clog shoes
comedy clubs
computer games
deck shoes
designer sweats
Dungeons and Dragons®
E.T. dolls
fanny packs
fifties clothing
flat-top haircut
flotation tanks
gourmet ice cream
Hacky Sack®
hand weights
home answering machines
jelly bean shoes
jogging
joysticks
lazer tag
leather bomber jackets

legwarmers
MTV
macramé friendship bracelets
music videos
Mutant Ninja Turtles®
New Wave music
oat bran
Pac Man
pasta
rap music
ripped jeans
rollerblade skates
Rubic's Cube
sequined T-shirts
skate boarding
slam dancing
Smurfs
snowboarding
square framed glasses
stress management seminars
sun porches
Susan B. Anthony dollar
suspenders
swatch watches
Trivial Pursuit®
tube dresses
valley girls
video dating services
walking shoes
wave, the
YUPPIES

237. Greeting Customs

handshake
high five
hugs
bowing
curtsey
nod
tipping one's hat
military salute

238. Rites of Passage

baptism
bar mitzvah
birthday cakes
birthday spankings
caps and gowns
circumcision
debutante balls
first communion
passing out cigars
retirement watch
sweet 16 party
vision quest

239. American Courtship Rituals & Customs

banns of marriage
bridal showers
bundling
chaperones
dating
diamonds
Dutch treat
engagement rings
flirting
kissing
parking
proposing on bended knee

240. American Wedding Rituals & Customs

bridal veil
bridesmaid
bride's parents pay
carrying bride over threshold
cutting the cake
decorating car
eloping
flower girls
garters
giving the bride away
groom
honeymoon
hope chests
June weddings
kissing the bride
throwing rice
trousseaus
wedding rings
white wedding dress

241. Funeral Rituals and Customs

coffins
embalming
flag at half mast
flowers
gun salutes
lighting candles
pall bearers
visitation at funeral home
wakes

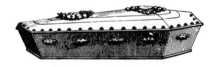

242. Traditional Castes of India

Highest to lowest:
Brahmans
Kshatriyas
Vaisyas
Sudras
Below the castes:
The untouchables

243. Anglo-American English Vocabulary

England and America are two people separated by a common language.

George Bernard Shaw

Anglo	American
aerodrome	airfield
bags	trousers
barrister	attorney
beaker	cup
bobby	police officer
bonnet	hood of a car
boot	car's trunk
braces	suspenders
car park	auto parking lot
chemist	pharmacist
chips	French fries
clatter	to gossip
conk	nose
elastoplast	bandaid
estate car	station wagon
first floor	second floor
flat	apartment
jumper	sweater
gaffer	shop foreman
Girl Guide	Girl Scout
gruel	oatmeal
gum	paste, glue
knock up	to awaken
larder	pantry

Anglo	American
let	to rent
lido	swimming pool
lift	elevator
litter bin	wastebasket
Ltd.	Inc.
lorry	truck
mackintosh	rain coat
mince	ground beef
motorway	highway
net ball	basketball
paper blind	window shade
petrol	gasoline
private hire	taxi
public school	private school
rambler	hiker
ring up	to telephone
round	sandwich
scurf	dandruff
serviette	napkin
singlet	T-shirt
squib	firecracker
state school	public school
telephonist	telephone operator
telly	TV
tin	can
W.C.	toilet
wind cheater	windbreaker

244. Citizens Band Radio Slang

Slang	Meaning	Slang	Meaning
affirmative	yes	lettuce	money
back off	slow down	log some Z's	to sleep
Bean Town	Boston	modulate	to talk
bear	law enforcement officer	negatory	no
bear bait	a speeder	over	end of transmission, done
bear in the air	highway patrol in airplane	Polaroid	police radar
bear in the grass	high patrol in median	pumpkin	flat tire
blinkin' winkin'	school bus	road tar	cup of coffee
breaker	interruption to talk on CB	smokey	highway patrol officer
		super slab	highway
		takin' pictures	using radar gun
come again	repeat last transmission	ten-four	yes, okay
double nickel	55 miles per hour	10-20	location
eighteen wheeler	semi, truck	threes	greetings
fluff stuff	snow	two-wheeler	motorcycle
good buddy	friend	wall-to-wall	crowded
handle	one's CB name	work twenty	where one works
hole in the wall	tunnel		
jockey	truck driver	Z's	sleep
land line	telephone		

245. The Golden Rule in Many Religions

Hurt not others with that which pains thyself.
  Buddhism

Whatsoever ye would that men should do to you, do ye even so to them.
  Christianity

What you don't want done to yourself, don't do to others.
  Confucianism

Do naught to others which if done to thee would cause pain.
  Hinduism

What is hateful to yourself, don't do to your fellow man.
  Judaism

May I do to others as I would that they should do unto me.
  Paganism (Plato)

Treat others as thou wouldst be treated theyself.
  Sikhism

Do not do unto others all that which is not well for oneself.
  Zoroastrianism

246. Religious Symbols

agnus dei	menorah
botonée	om
Celtic cross	papal cross
chalice	patriarchal cross
dove	Russian cross
Greek cross	shiva
Jerusalen cross	star and cresant
Latin cross	Star of David
lotus	tau cross
Maltese cross	torii
mandala	yin-yang

247. Holy Books

Holy Book	Religion
Bhagavad-Gita	Hinduism
Five Classics	Confucianism
Koran	Islam
New Testament	Christianity
Old Testament	Judaism & Christianity
Torah	Judaism
Talmud	Judaism
Tao-te-ching	Taoism
Upanishads	Hinduism
Veda	Hinduism

248. Major Causes of Death in the United States

(In approximate order of frequency)
cardiovascular disease
cancer
pneumonia
motor vehicle accidents
other accidents
diabetes
congenital anomaly
cirrosis of the liver
suicides
homicide
nephritis and nephrosis
hernia and intestinal obstructions

249. Words Borrowed from African Languages

banana
banjo
bogus
boogie
bug
dig
fuzz
goober
gumbo
guy

hippie
jam
jamboree
mumbo jumbo
okra
phony
tote
voodoo

250. Common Words Borrowed from Spanish

adobe
aficionado
alfalfa
alligator
armada
arroyo
banana
barbecue
breeze
bronco
buffalo
burro
cabana
cafeteria
calaboose
canary
canyon
cargo
chaparral
chili
chocolate
cigar
cocaine
cockroach
corral
coyote
desperado

filibuster
guerrilla
hammock
incommunicado
junta
lariat
lasso
macho
maize
marijuana
mesa
mesquite
patio
peon
plaza
portal
pueblo
ranch
rodeo
savvy
siesta
tabasco
tapioca
tobacco
tornado
tortilla
vanilla
vigilante

251. Australian Slang

Slang	Meaning
aeroplanes	bow tie
air and exercise	short jail term
Arry gators	thanks
Aussie	an Australian
bad dog	overdue debt
barbie	barbeque
barney over	quarrel
battler	a persistent loser
beano	a fun party
bloke	man
bludger	someone who doesn't do their fair share
blue	a fight
bush	a rural area
chalkie	teacher
crook	defective; sick
dill	a fool
dingo	Australian wild dog
dole bludger	welfare cheat
drongo	a super dill; big fool
drover	cowboy
the dry	annual nine month drought
fair dinkum	true blue; loyal
flat out	full speed; very fast
flying doe	female kangaroo
galah	silly and dull
garbo	garbage man
gin	aborigine woman
good on you	good for you (sometimes sarcastic)
have kangaroos in your top paddock	to be crazy
jackeroo	cowboy
jillaroo	cowgirl
jumper	sweater
kangarooster	odd person
mozzies	mosquitoes
outback	Australian back country
paddock	field or pasture
postie	postal worker

Slang	Meaning
ringer	cowboy
ripper	great! excellent!
sheila	woman
shot through	went home
skite	to brag; boast
smoko	rest period; a break
squatter	landed gentry
station	cattle ranch
stone the crows	exclamation of surprise or disgust
strewth	It's the truth
swag	bedroll for traveling light
take a sickie	stay home for any reason other than illness
to do your block	to lose your temper
tooright	You're so right!
too end	extreme north of Australia
tucker	meal, food
the wet	three-month rainy season
value for money	a good man
you bewdy	you're okay; exclamation of approval

252. Words Borrowed from Native Americans

caucus	powwow
Chautaugua	quahog
chipmunk	raccoon
hickory	Sequoia
hogan	skunk
hominy	squash
igloo	squaw
moccasin	succotash
moose	tepee
muskrat	totem
opossum	toboggan
papoose	tomahawk
pecan	wahoo
pemmican	wampum
persimmon	wigwam
podunk	woodchuck

253. Contemporary Social Problems

AIDS
Aging population with inadequate health care
Continued racism
Cost of medical care
The cycle of poverty
Date rape
Drug and alcohol abuse
Environmental pollution
Excessive school drop-out rate
Growth in the crime rate
High unemployment among black youth
High rates of teenage pregancies
Illiteracy
Increased trends in suicide
Increasing child abuse
Plight of the farmers
Poor educational achievement
Proliferation of firearms and violence
Sexual harassment and sex discrimination
Teenage run-aways
Threat of international terrorism
High numbers of homeless persons
Violence in the streets

254. Southern Foods

awendaw	iced tea
beignets	jambalayas
bell peppers	key lime pie
biscuits	mint julip
black-eyed peas	molasses
cabbage	muddle
calas	mutton burgoo
collards	okra
corncakes	oyster pie
cornbread	peanut soup
cowpeas	pecan pie
cracklins	persimmons
crawfish	pokeweed
cymlings	pork rinds
dumplings	pralines
eggplant	rice
figs	seafood
fried chicken	shoofly pie
grits	sorgum molasses pie
gumbo	spoon bread
ham	sweet potatoes
hoecakes	turnips
hush puppies	Virginia baked ham

255. Notable Hispanic Americans

Jerry Apodaca	New Mexico Governor, 1974-79
Donna Alvardo	Director of ACTION, government agency
Herman Badillo	U.S. Congressman from New York
Joan Baez	popular protest song recording artist
Romana A. Bañuelos	U.S. Treasurer, 1971-74
Raymond Barrio	author
Nash Candelaria	author
Vickki Carr	popular singer
Lauro Cavazos	Secretary of Education
César Chavez	labor leader
Henry G. Cisneros	Mayor of San Antonio
Roberto Clemente	baseball player
Jaime Escalante	Los Angeles teacher who inspired the movie, *Stand and Deliver*
Freddy Fender	singer
Hector Garcia	U.S. Civil Rights Commissioner
Henry B. Gonzales	First Mexican-American congressman
Rodolfo "Corky" Gonzales	boxing champion, Democratic party leader
José Gutiérrez	organized "La Rasa Unida", political third party
Marí-Luci Jaramillo	U.S. ambassador to Honduras
Luis Jiménez	muralist, sculptor
Joe Kapp	professional football player
Nancy Lopez	women's professional golfer
Trini Lopez	popular singer
Manuel Lujan, Jr.	U.S. Representative, Secretary of Interior
Bob Martinez	Govenor of Florida
Elba Molina	prominent Arizona businesswoman
Joseph Montoyo	first Mexican-American Senator (New Mexico)
Katherine Davalos Ortega	U.S. Treasurer
Anthony Quinn	Successful actor
Belinda Cárdenas Ramírez	first woman appointed to the Civil Rights Commission
Diego Rivera	muralist
Linda Ronstadt	singer
Gary Soto	writer
Manuel Hernández Trujillo	artist
Richie Valens	singer
Richard Vásquez	author of *The Plam Plum Pickers*
Esteban Villa	painter
José Antonio Villareal	author of *Poncho* and other works

256. Notable Arab Americans

F. Murray Abraham	actor, won Oscar for *Amadeus*
George Addes	secretary-treasurer of United Auto Workers
Mansour Farah	clothing manufacturer (Farah Company)
Jamie Farr	actor; Corporal Klinger from *M*A*S*H*
Doug Flutie	pro football player
Kahlil Gibran	author of *The Prophet*
Theodore Gontos	clothing retailer
Phillip Habib	under secretary of state for political affairs
Joseph Haggar	clothing manufacturer (Haggar Company)
John Kacere	artist
Casey Kasem	radio and television personality
Ralph Nader	consumer advocate
Rosa Lee Nemir	medical researcher
Mary Rose Oakar	U.S. Congresswoman
Donna Shalala	college president
Marlo Thomas	actress
Helen Thomas	White House press corps journalist

257. Things Not Around in 1960

acrylic paint
aeorbics
affirmative action programs
AIDS
air bags
airport metal detectors
alkaline batteries
alkyd paint
aluminum softball bats
Amtrak
Apple Computer
area codes
artificial hearts
astroturf
athletic scholarships for women
automatic garage door openers
automatic teller machines
bagelinos
bar codes
Beatles, The
Berlin Wall
Bic pens
bug zappers
cable vision
call forwarding
cassette auto tapes
catalytic converters
Catholic church services in English
cellular phones
cigarette package warnings
clear braces
compact discs
computerized tomography (CAT scan)
consumer price index
cubic zirconium diamonds
Department of Education
Department of Energy

designer jeans
digital audio tape
disposable diapers
disposable razors
DNA fingerprinting
dolby noise reduction system
drug education programs
Earth Day
electric toothbrush
express mail
extended wear contact lenses
fanny packs
fathers in the delivery room
female astronauts
female coal miners
female secret service agents
fiber optics
food processors
food stamps
frequent flyer programs
frozen yogurt
garbage disposals
gene cloning
glosnot
graphite tennis racquets
hang gliders
Head Start programs
heart pacemakers
heart transplants
holograms
home computers
home VCR's
hot air poppers
indoor soccer
instamatic cameras
instant replay
jet skis

257. Things Not Around in 1960, continued

laser surgery
legal abortions
liquid crystal display (LCD)
Martin Luther King Day
Mastercharge Cards
MTV
medicare
microwave ovens
Moscow "hot line"
music synthesizer
national voting age of 18
911 emergency number
National Organization for Women
neutron bombs
1-800 telephone numbers
1-900 telephone numbers
"no fault" divorce
non-smoking sections
orthoscopic surgery
Peace Corps
permanent press slacks
phosphate-free detergents
plastic garbage bags
pocket calculators
political action committees (PAC's)
push-button telephones
quartz digital watches
radial tires
radioactive waste
rechargeable flashlights
remote control
revoling restaurants
robots
scanners
seat belts
self-serve gas stations
skateboards
smart bombs

smoke detectors
soft contact lenses
sun roofs
supertankers
space shuttle
sports dome
Star Trek
stereophonic radio broadcasts
styling mousse
styrofoam
Super Bowl
supersonic transport planes
surrogate mothers
synthetic skin
talking cars
televised congressional sessions
TV instant replay
test tube babies
three-point shots in basketball
touch-tone telephones
twist-ties
two-liter plastic soda bottles
USA Today
unit pricing in supermarkets
valium
video arcades
waterbeds
windsurfing
word processors
ZIP codes

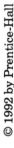

258. Things from 1960 That Are Hard to Find Today

asbestos
auto tire inner tubes
autumn leaf fires
bakelite
black and white television programs
Burma Shave signs
car hops
chrome automobile bumpers
cigarette smoking on airplanes
drive-in theaters
Edsels
elm trees
flash bulbs
free air at gas stations
free maps at gas stations
48-star flags
glass milk bottles
Gulf Oil Corporation
home delivery bread men
home delivery milk men
home movie cameras
Look magazine
manual typewriter
"men wanted" classified ads
military draft
motor scooters
New York Herald Tribune
penny gumball machines
PCB's
percolators
poll taxes
prayers in public schools
prefrontal lobotomies
push lawn mowers
ringer washers
rotary telephones
78 rpm records
shaving brushes

silver in U.S. coins
slide rules
smallpox vaccinations
stenographers
Studebakers
Sunday "Blue" laws
29¢ per gallon gasoline
telephone party lines
TV cigarette ads
Thalidomide
toothpaste powder
vacuum tube
"wheat" pennies
"whites only" signs
wood tennis racquets

259. Forms of American Music

acid rock
big band

bluegrass
blues
Cajun
country & western
crooners
folk
folk rock
gospel
Hawaiian
heavy metal
"hillbilly"
honkey-tonk
jazz
motown sound
new wave
protest
punk
ragtime
rap
religious
rock and roll
rhythm and blues
sacred harp
soul
spirituals
swing
"Tex-Mex"
western swing
zydeco

260. Traditional Wedding Anniversaries

Year	Gift
First	Paper
Second	Cotton
Third	Leather
Fourth	Linen
Fifth	Wooden
Sixth	Iron
Seventh	Copper
Eighth	Bronze
Ninth	Pottery
Tenth	Tin
Fifteenth	Crystal
Twentieth	China
Twenty-fifth	Silver
Thirtieth	Ivory
Fortieth	Woolen
Forty-fifth	Sapphire
Fiftieth	Gold
Sixtieth	Diamond
Seventy-fifth	Diamond

261. Forms of Marriage

Monogamy	marriage of one man and one woman
Polygamy	men having more than one wife
Polyandry	women having more than one husband
Exogamy	prohibition of marriage to one's relatives
Endogamy	marriage only permitted to a member of one's own family

262. American Indian Medical Remedies

Ailment	Remedy
acne	wild bergamot
asthma	skunk cabbage, jimson weed
athlete's foot	yellow nut grass tubers
bad breath	geranium roots
bee stings	tobacco
blisters	sunflower roots
boils	wild pansies
bronchitis	creosote bush tea
burns	yellow-spined thistle salve, black alder
childbirth pain	wild black cherry
colds	wintergreen
colic	catnip
coughs	aspen bark, sarsaparilla roots
diarrhea	blackberry tea, white oak bark
dysentery	magnolia bark
earache	licorice leaves, ginger
fevers	bayberry, white poplar bark
flu	evergreen frest hemlock
headaches	skunk cabbage
insect bites	wild onion or garlic bulbs, snakeweed
measles	sassafras roots
mumps	sweet everlasting; red cedar tea
poison ivy	gum plant, wormwood
ringworm	red birch, mulberry
stomachache	dandelion tea, snowberry
snake bite	Virginia snakeroot, Beneca snakeroot
sore throat	white pine needles tea, slippery elm tea
stop bleeding	puffballs, wild geranium root
toothache	prickly ash bark
swelling	witch hazel, blue flag (iris) root

263. Advice from Aesop

Wise men say nothing in dangerous times.

Quality comes before quantity.

Slow and steady wins the race.

One man's meat is another man's poison.

Look before you leap.

Figures are not always facts.

It is one thing to propose, another to execute.

Acts speak plainer than words.

Necessity is the mother of invention.

Men are blind to their own faults.

There is no arguing a coward into courage.

Grasp at the shadow and lose the substance.

One good turn deserves another.

Nip evil in the bud. Spare the rod and spoil the child.

Honesty is the best policy.

Union is strength.

Keep to your place and your place will keep to you.

Example is better than precept.

The lights of heaven are never blown out.

Revenge is too dearly purchased at the price of liberty.

There can be little liking where there is little likeness.

A bird in the hand is worth two in the bush.

He who plays a trick must be prepared to take a joke.

264. Major World Religions

Buddhism
Christianity
Hinduism
Islam
Judaism

265. Ivy League Colleges

Brown, 1764
Columbia, 1754
Cornell, 1865
Dartmouth, 1769
Harvard, 1636
Pennsylvania, 1740
Princeton, 1746
Yale, 1701

266. Seven Sisters

Barnard, 1889
Bryn Mawr, 1885
Mount Holyoke, 1837
Radcliff, 1879
Smith, 1871
Vassar, 1861
Wellsley, 1875

267. Major U.S. Disasters

Epidemic, over 30,000 die	1618-23
East coast hurricane, over 4,000 die	1775
Cholera epidemic, thousands die	1832
Steamboat *Sultana* explodes; over 1,500 die	1865
Massive forest fires, Michigan, Minnesota, Wisconsin	1871
Chicago fire	1871
Brooklyn Conway Theatre fire	1876
Massive blizzard	1888
Johnstown, Pennsylvania, flood	1889
Hurricane, over 1,000 die	1893
Galveston hurricane, over 6,000 die	1900
Chicago's second fire	1906
San Francisco earthquake	1906
Monograph, West Virginia coal mine	1907
New Madrid, Missouri earthquake	1911
Titanic sinks	1912
Luisitania sinks	1915
Steamer *Eastland* sinks in Chicago River	1915
Forest fire, Wisconsin & Minnesota	1918
Spanish flu epidemic, 500,000 die	1918
San Paulo, Colorado, dam collapse	1928
South Florida hurricane	1928
Hurricane of '38, over 600 die	1938
Boston's Coconut Grove nightclub fire	1942
Two navy ammo ships explode, Port Chicago, California	1944
Freighter *Grandcamp* explodes, 561 die	1947
Hurricane Diane	1955
AIDS epidemic, over 100,000 dead	1980's

268. Annual American Celebrations

New Year's Day
Martin Luther King's Birthday
Groundhog's Day
Valentine's Day
President's Day
Leap Year Day
St. Patrick's Day
Mardi Gras
Ash Wednesday
April Fool's Day
Easter Sunday
Passover
Mother's Day
Arbor Day
Memorial Day
Flag Day
Father's Day
Independence Day
Labor Day
Columbus Day
Halloween
Veterans' Day
Thanksgiving
Christmas
Boxing Day
New Year's Eve
birthdays
wedding anniversaries

269. Performers at Woodstock

Joan Baez	Tim Hardin	Quill
The Band	Keef Hartley	Santana
Jeff Beck Group	Richie Havens	Ravi Shankar
Blood, Sweat and Tears	Jimi Hendrix	Sly and the Family Stone
Canned Heat	Incredible String Band	
Credence Clearwater	Iron Butterfly	Bert Sommer
Joe Cocker	Janis Joplin	Sweetwater
Crosby, Stills and Nash	Jefferson Airplane	Ten Years After
Grateful Dead	Mountain	The Who
Arlo Guthrie		Johnny Winter

270. Celebrity Deaths from Alleged Drug Overdoses

Len Bias	basketball player
John Belushi	comedian
Tommy Bolin	guitarist
John Bonham	member of "Led Zepplin"
Lenny Bruce	comedian
Tim Buckley	singer-songwriter
Brian Cole	member of "The Association"
Sandy Denny	singer
Brian Epstein	"Beatles" manager
Judy Garland	actress
Andy Gibb	singer
Tim Hardin	singer-songwriter
Jimi Hendrix	rock star
Billie Holiday	jazz singer
Brian Jones	member of "The Rolling Stones"
Little Willie John	singer
Janis Joplin	singer
Frankie Lymon	member of "The Teenagers"
Robbie McIntosh	"Average White Band" drummer
Aimee Semple McPherson	evangelist
Marilyn Monroe	actress
Pam Morrison	wife of Jim Morrison of "The Doors"
Keith Moon	member of "The Who"
Nico	member of "Velvet Underground"
Gram Parsons	member of "The Byrds"
Elvis Presley	rock star
David Ruffin	singer with The Temptations
Bon Scott	"AC/DC" singer
Rory Storme	rock musician
Vinnie Taylor	"Sha Na Na" guitarist
Gary Thain	"Uriah Heep" guitarist
Sid Vicious	member of "The Sex Pistols"
Danny Whitten	"Crazy Horse" singer-songwriter
Al Wilson	member of "Canned Heat"
Dennis Wilson	member of "The Beach Boys"

271. Countries Prohibiting Capital Punishment

Australia
Austria
Bolivia
Columbia
Costa Rica
Denmark
Dominican Republic
Ecuador
Finland
France
Germany
Haiti
Honduras
Iceland
Liechtenstein

Luxembourg
Netherlands
Nicaragua
Norway
Panama
Philippines
Portugal
Solomon Islands
Sweden
Uruguay
Venezuela

272. States Prohibiting Capital Punishment

Alaska
Hawaii
Iowa
Kansas
Maine
Massachusetts
Michigan
Minnesota
New York
North Dakota
Vermont
West Virginia
Wisconsin

273. The Risks of Cocaine Use

damage to the heart muscle
paralysis of breathing muscles
hypertension
chest pain
liver damage
irregularities in the heart beat
cerebral hemorrhage
bronchitis
heart attacks
hyperthermia
strokes

274. Warning Signs of Alcohol Abuse

drinking as an immediate response to any problem
all celebrations must include alcohol
driving a car while intoxicated
sleep disturbances
blackouts
using alcohol to handle any stress
missing school or work because of drinking
drinking until intoxicated

275. Drug Abuse Danger Signals

sudden change in mood
possession of drug paraphernalis
unusual temper outbursts
abrupt change in friends
increased absence from school or work
stealing from others
increased borrowing of money
sudden increase in behavioral problems
poor relationships with parents or friends

276. Largest American Indian Tribes

Cherokee
Navajo
Sioux
Chippewa
Choctaw
Pueblo
Iroquois
Apache
Lumbee
Creek

277. Predictors of Successful Marriages

both partners had a happy childhood
both sets of parents were successfully married
both are emotionally well adjusted
both had good relationships with their parents
high self-esteem in both partners
healthy instruction in human sexuality
of similar religious beliefs
couple dated at least a year
bride is at least 19 and groom at least 22
relatively similar educational backgrounds

278. American Sports Firsts

game of baseball invented by Abner Doubleday	1839
baseball team (Knickerbocker Club)	1845
yacht race	1845
America's Cup yacht race	1851
cricket match (Hoboken, N.J.)	1859
intercollegiate baseball game (Amherst vs. Williams College)	1859
football club (Boston)	1862
women's baseball team	1868
intercollegiate football game (Princeton vs. Rutgers)	1869
professional baseball player (Alfred Reach)	1871
baseball glove	1875
tennis court (Boston)	1876
croquet league (Philadelphia)	1880
bareknuckle world heavyweight championship (Paddy Ryan)	1880
lawn tennis championship	1881
night baseball game	1883
basketball game invented by James Naismith	1892
college basketball team (Mt. Union College)	1892
night football game (Mansfield, Pa.)	1892
18 hole golf course (Wheaton, Ill.)	1893
professional football game	1895
volleyball invented by W. G. Morgan	1895
modern Olympic games started (Athens, Greece)	1896
professional hockey team	1903
world series baseball game (Pittsburgh Pirates beat Boston Americans)	1903
squash tournament	1911
PGA golf championship	1916
curling rink (Brookline, Mass.)	1920
American Badminton Association founded	1936
Super Bowl football game	1967

279. Values

achievement
beauty
bravery
cleanliness
considerateness
cooperation
creativity
diligence
equality
exciting life
family
forgiveness
freedom
friendship
generosity
happiness
hard worker
health
intelligence
justice
kindness
lasting contribution
love

loyalty
national security
obedience
openmindedness
order
peace
perseverance
pleasure
power
rationality
recognition
responsibility
salvation
security
self-reliance
self-respect
success
thoughtfulness
tradition
truth
wealth
wisdom

280. Possible Purposes of Schools

To develop skills for work
To learn how to manage money and resources
To learn how to use leisure time
To appreciate beauty
To learn the rules and expectations of the culture
To develop an ethical character
To develop one's abilities to the fullest
To select a career
To develop effective work habits and values
To develop positive self-esteem
To develop good health habits
To become responsible citizens
To learn how to be a worthy family member
To understand and get along with others
To develop basic skills in reading, writing, and
    mathematics
To learn the skills of effective decision making
To help solve the social problems (e.g., poverty, racism, pollution)

281. Sociology Related Journals

Administration in Social Work
The American Journal of Drug and Alcohol Abuse
Behavior Therapy
Child and Adolescent Social Work Journal
Child and Youth Services
Child Welfare
Clinical Social Work Journal
Community Mental Health Journal
Crisis Intervention
Gerontologist
Health and Social Work
Hospice Journal
Indian Journal of Social Work
International Social Work
Intervention
Journal of Divorce
Journal of Independent Social Work
Journal of Marriage and Family
Journal of Social Work and Human Sexuality
Journal of Sociology and Social Welfare
Parenting Studies
Prevention in Human Services
Public Welfare
School Social Work Journal
Small Group Behavior
Social Work
Social Work Research and Abstracts
Social Work Today
Society
Sociology and Social Research
Suicide and Life-Threatening Behavior
Urban and Social Change Review
Youth and Society

Section VI

LISTS FOR PSYCHOLOGY

282. Fields of Psychology

adolescent development
animal
behavioral pharmacology
child
clinical
cognitive
community
comparative
consulting
consumer
counseling
developmental
educational
engineering
evaluation and measurement
experimental

forensic
genetic
history of psychology
industrial
learning
military
organizational
personality
philosophical
physiological
psycholinguistics
psychometrics
psychopathology
rehabilitation
school psychology
social

283. Careers in Psychology and Mental Health

career counselor
child psychologist
clinical psychologist
cognitive psychologist
community mental health aid
counseling psychologist
counselor
educational psychologist
group home supervisor
high school psychology teacher
human resource development
industrial psychologist
intake interviewer
marriage counselor
mental health research
organizational consultant
pastoral counselor
probation officer
professor
psychometrician
research technician
school psychologist
social psychologist
substance abuse counselor
test developer
training and development consultant

284. Eminent Pioneer Psychologists

Anne Anastasi
Albert Bandura
Alfred Binet
Mary W. Calkins
Walter Cannon
Raymond Cattell
Maine de Biran
John Dewey
Dorothea Dix
June Etta Downey
Hermann Ebbinghaus
Erik Erikson
Gustav Fechner
Leon Festinger
Arnold Gesell
G. Stanley Hall
Hermann Helmholtz

Mary Henle
Clark Hull
Kurt Kofka
William James
George Kelly
Wolfgang Köhler
Abraham Maslow
Maria Montessori
Ivan Pavlov
Jean Piaget
Carl Rogers
B. F. Skinner
Lewis Terman
Edward Titchener
E. L. Thorndike
Leona Tyler

285. Prominent Figures in the History of Psychiatry

Alfred Adler
Ruth Benedict
Eugen Bleuler
Abraham Brill
Helene Deutsch
Sigmund Freud
Anna Freud
Erich Fromm
Wilhelm Griesinger
Karen Horney
Carl Jung
Thomas Kirkbride
Melanie Klein
Emil Kraepelin

Rollo May
Philippe Pinel
Otto Rank
Harry S. Sullivan
E. B. Titchener

286. Phobias

phobia	abnormal fear of . . .	phobia	abnormal fear of . . .
acrophobia	high places	isophobia	poison
agoraphobia	open spaces	kakorrhaphiophobia	failure or defeat
aichmophobia	sharp instruments	leukophobia	color white
ailurophobia	cats	linonophobia	string
amathophobia	dust	menophobia	being alone
anthophobia	flowers	microphobia	germs
anthropophobia	people	murophobia	mice
aphephobia	touch	mysophobia	dirt
arachnophobia	spiders	nyctophobia	dark
astraphobia	lightening	ochlophobia	crows
ataxiophobia	disorder	ochophobia	riding in cars
aulophobia	flutes	ombrophobia	rain
blennophobia	slime	ophidiophobia	snakes
brontophobia	thunder	parthenophobia	young girls
bymnophobia	nudity	phobophobia	fear
cathisophobia	sitting down	phonophobia	noise
claustrophobia	closed places	photophobia	light
crystallophobia	glass	phrenophobia	going insane
cynophobia	dogs	phronemophobia	thinking
dromophobia	crossing streets	pnigophobia	choking
entomophobia	insects	pyrophobia	fire
equinophobia	horses	rhypophobia	filth
frigophobia	cold	scriptophobia	writing in public
galeophobia	sharks	thanatophobia	death
gamophobia	marriage	theophobia	god
gephyrophobia	crossing a bridge	tonitrophobia	thunder
geumophobia	flavors	trichophobia	hair
harpaxophobia	being robbed	triskaidekaphobia	the number 13
hedonophobia	sunlight	uranophobia	homosexuality
heliophobia	pleasure	vermiphobia	worms
hydrophobia	water; rabies	xenophobia	strangers
hygrophobia	liquids	zoophobia	animals
iatrophobia	doctors		

287. Counseling Approaches

Theory	Primary Proponent
Action Therapy	O'Connell
Actualizing Therapy	Shostrum
Adlerian Individual Psychotherapy	Adler
Art Therapy	
Assertion-Structured Therapy	Phillips
Attack Therapy	Synanon
Aversion Therapy	
Behavioral Marital Therapy	Jacobson & Margolin
Behavioral Therapy	Wolpe
Bibliotherapy	Gottschalk
Biocentric Therapy	
Bioenergetic Therapy	Reich
Brief Therapy	Smal; Alexander & French
Character Analysis Therapy	Horney
Client-Centered Therapy	Rogers
Cognitive Behavior Modification	Meichenbaum
Cognitive Therapy	Beck
Conjoint Family Therapy	Satir
Conjoint Sex Therapy	Masters & Johnson
Construct Counseling	
Correspondence Therapy	Parsons
Dance Therapy	Chace
Decision Counseling	Greenwald
Directive Psychotherapy	Thorne
Eclectic Models of Counseling	Egan
Ego Psychotherapy	Federn & Weiss
Existential Therapy	May, Bugenthal
Experimental Therapy	Whitaker & Malone
Family Systems Therapy	Bowen
Freudian Psychoanalysis	Freud
Functional Family Therapy	Barton & Alexander
Gestalt Therapy	Perls
Hypnotherapy	Milton Erickson
Intensive Journal Process	Progroff
Jungian Analytical Psychotherapy	Jung
Learning Theory Psychotherapy	Dollard and Miller
Logotherapy	Frankl
Marital Counseling	Mudd, Stone & Stone
Massed-time Therapy	Ries
Milan Systemic Family Therapy	Selvini-Palazzoli
Milieu Therapy	Pinel, Rush
Modern Psychoanalysis	Spotnitz
Multimodal Behavioral Therapy	Lazarus
Music Therapy	
Multiple Impact Therapy	McGregor

287. Counseling Approaches, continued

Theory	Primary Proponent
Multiple Family Therapy	Laqueur
Narcotherapy	
Object Relations Therapy	Kohut
Objective Psychotherapy	Karpman
Occupational Therapy	
Orgone Therapy	Reich
Operant Interpersonal Therapy	Stuart
Pastoral Counseling	Boisen
Philosophical Psychotherapy	
Play Therapy	Axline
Poetry Therapy	
Primal Therapy	Janov
Provocative Therapy	Farrelly
Psycho-Imagination Therapy	Shorr
Psychosynthesis	Tien
Psychodrama	Moreno
Rational Emotive Therapy	Albert Ellis
Recreational Therapy	
Relaxation Therapy	Kraines, Jacobson
Re-evaluation Counseling	Jackens
Relationship Therapy	Patterson
Release Therapy	Levy
Sector Therapy	Deutsch
Sex Therapy	Masters and Johnson
Social Learning Therapy	Bandura
Solution-Focused Brief Therapy	de Shazer
Strategic Family Therapy	Madanes & Haley
Structural Family Therapy	Minuchin
Supportive Therapy	Watkins
Supportive-Expressive Psychotherapy	Luborsky
Symbolic-Experimental Family Therapy	
Time-Limited Dynamic Therapy	Strupp and Binder
Total Push Therapy	Myerson
Transactional Analysis	Berne
Transpersonal Psychology	

288. Psychotherapeutic Techniques

bibliotherapy
confrontation
directives
dream analysis
free association
homework
hypnosis
interpretation
paraphrasing
persuasion
projective tests
psychodrama
questioning
reflection of feelings
rehearsal
relaxation training
role playing
silence
suggestion
systematic desensitization
testing

289. Commonly Used Psychological Tests

Wechsler Adult Intelligence Scale, Revised (WAIS-R)
Minnesota Multiphasic Personality Inventory (MMPI)
Thematic Apperception Test (TAT)
Rorschach Test
Myers-Briggs Type Indicator
Draw-a-Person Test (DAP)
House-Tree-Person Test (HTP)
Wechsler Intelligence Scale for Children, Revised (WISC-R)
Peabody Picture Vocabulary Test (PPVT)
Bender-Gestalt Visual Motor Test
Stanford-Binet Intelligence Test

290. Types of Tests

achievement
aptitude
attitude
intelligence
interest inventories
personality
projective

291. Famous People Who Did Poorly in School

Winston Churchill was one of the worst students in his class. He was branded as careless and unpunctual by his headmaster. He won the Nobel Prize for Literature in 1953.

Thomas Edison was labeled by his teachers as "too stupid to learn." He attended grammar school for only three months because his teachers considered him to be "addled."

Albert Einstein did not talk until he was four, nor read until age nine. He failed a math course. The first time he tried, he failed his entrance examination at Polytechnic Institute in Zurich. He was judged to have "no promise."

William Faulkner was briefly enrolled in Ole Miss. He received a "D" in English.

Isaac Newton flunked mathematics in school.

Carl Sandburg, the poet, flunked out of West Point, supposedly because of "deficiencies in English."

Albert Schweitzer's mother would cry because he received such poor grades.

Woodrow Wilson did not learn his letters until he was nine years old or to read until he was eleven.

Émile Zola once received a zero in French literature and composition.

292. Characteristics of Successful Persons

From extensive study of outstanding achievers a number of researchers have arrived at traits which tend to be possessed by successful persons.

Are committed to their goals
Are able to set priorities
Have learned how to learn
Are results oriented
Continually seek new challenges
Manage stress effectively
Focus upon a mission
Learn how to make decisions
Practice mental rehearsal
Take calculated risks
Maintain flexibility
Ask for what they want
Are able to ask the right questions
Keep their promises
Are good listeners
Can tolerate rejection and loss

Practice persistence
Avoid perfectionism
Accept help from successful people
Trust their hunches
Are able to negotiate
Anticipate what can go wrong
Feel good about themselves
Strive to improve
Practice patience
Are assertive when necessary
Are honest
Are able to see the other person's point of view
Avoid self-pity
Use praise more than criticism
Learn to say no
Trust themselves

293. Initial Failures

Burt Reynolds and **Clint Eastwood** were both fired by the same studio on the same day. The opinion was that neither had star potential.

Fred Smith, the founder of Federal Express, lost a million dollars a month for the first two years.

Candice Bergen flunked out of the University of Pennsylvania.

Jerry West was supposedly such a poor basketball player as a boy that other boys would not let him join their games.

Babe Ruth was the New York Yankees' second choice to play right field.

Henry Ford was broke at the age of 40.

Chevy Chase was expelled from Haverford College. He transferred to Bard College.

Vince Lombardi, one of the most outstanding professional football coaches, was a line coach at Fordham University at the age of 43.

Abraham Lincoln was twice defeated in his bid for the U.S. Senate.

Buckminster Fuller was twice expelled from Harvard.

Michael Douglas flunked out of the University of California.

Chester A. Arthur, twenty-first president of the United States, was fired as collector of the port of New York.

William Kennedy's book, *Ironweed*, was rejected by 13 publishers. He later won the Pulitzer Prize for his novel.

Benjamin Harrison was defeated for governor of Indiana and the United States Senate before being elected President of the United States.

Theodore Roosevelt was defeated in his bid for mayor of New York City.

James K. Polk, the eleventh president, was twice defeated for governor of Tennessee.

Joe Namath's SAT scores were too low for admission to the University of Maryland. He ended up as an award-winning quarterback at the University of Alabama before entering the professional ranks.

William Faulkner was turned down for membership by a literary society at Ole Miss.

Michael Jordan was cut from his high school basketball team his junior year.

Fred Astaire was evaluated by one casting director as "can't act, slightly bald, can dance a little . . ."

Lucille Ball failed her first drama class. The teacher asserted that Lucille "had no talent."

Lee Iacocca was turned down for a scholarship at Purdue.

Calvin Coolidge was defeated for a school board in Northampton, Massachusetts, prior to his election to the presidency.

Eleanor Roosevelt fainted the first time she tried to speak in public.

Richard Bach's best selling book *Jonathan Livingston Seagull* was turned down by two dozen publishers.

Abraham Lincoln's 1863 Gettysburg Address was judged by *The Chicago Times* as ". . . loose-joined, so puerile, not alone in literary construction, but in its ideas, its sentiments, its grasp. He has outdone himself. He has literally come out of the little end of his own horn. By the side of it, mediocrity is superb."

Robert Pirig's bestselling book, *Zen and the Art of Motorcycle Maintenance*, was rejected by 121 publishers before it was finally accepted.

The Duke of Windsor, the future King Edward VIII of England, failed his entrance exam into the Royal Navy.

Thomas Edison unsuccessfully tried 50,000 different elements for his lightbulb before finding the one which worked.

294. Famous Persons Who Were Learning-Disabled

Hans Christian Andersen
Cher
Winston Churchill
Tom Cruise
Leonardo da Vinci
Walt Disney
Thomas Edison
Albert Einstein

Bruce Jenner
Greg Louganis
George Patton
Nelson Rockefeller
O. J. Simpson
Woodrow Wilson
F. W. Woolworth

295. Views of Success

Success is going from failure to failure without loss of enthusiasm.
—Winston Churchill

If there is one secret of success it lies in the ability to get the other person's point of view and see things from his angle as well as your own. —Henry Ford

Self-trust is the first secret of success. —Ralph Waldo Emerson

I don't know the key to success; but the key to failure is trying to please everybody.
—Bill Cosby

When I was a young man I observed that nine out of ten things I did were failures. I didn't want to be a failure, so I did ten times more work.
—George Bernard Shaw

The secret to success in any human endeavor is total concentration.
—Kurt Vonnegut, author

There is a simple formula for success, and I'll tell what it is; Always do more than you're paid to do. —Sidney Sheldon, author

There are two ways to climb an oak tree. You can climb it, or you can sit on an acorn.
—Zig Ziglar, motivational speaker

You become the champion by fighting one more round.
—James J. Corbett, heavyweight champion

If you wish to succeed in life, make perseverance your bosom friend, experience your wise counselor, caution your elder brother, and hope your guardian genius.
—Joseph Addison

Try not to become a man (sic) of success but rather try to become a man of value.
—Albert Einstein

A man is a success if he gets up in the morning and gets to bed at night, and in between he does what he wants to do. —Bob Dylan

Never continue in a job you don't enjoy. If you're happy in what you're doing, you'll like yourself, you'll have inner peace. And if you have that, along with physical health, you will have had more success that you could possibly have imagined.
—Johnny Carson

296. Physiological Needs

appropriate body temperature
elimination of body wastes
food
oxygen
pain avoidance
physical activity
sensory stimulation
sex
sleep and rest
water

297. Psychological Needs

achievement
affiliation
aggression
approval of others
attention
avoidance of embarrassment
avoidance of unpleasant experiences
control; power
creativity; expression
dependence
dominance
fun
knowledge
independence
love
nurturance
orderliness
recognition
revenge
security
self-actualization
self-esteem
sex

298. Common Defense Mechanisms

compensation
denial of reality
displacement
fantasy
fixation
intellectualization
introjection
overcompensation
projection
rationalization
reaction formation
regression
repression
sublimation

299. Early Treatments for Mental Illness

administration of hellebore
baths
beating
copious bleeding
dunking heads under water
electric shock
execution
exorcism
frontal lobotomy
hot irons applied to the head
insulin shock treatment
lowering afflicted into snake pits
shackling
spinning in a centrifuge
straitjackets
tossing afflicted from high cliffs
trephining (boring a hole in the skull)
tying up patient
wrapping in wet sheets

300. Psychology Firsts

mental asylums in the world (Baghdad; Damascus) c. 800
mental hospital in Europe (Valencia, Spain) 1409
mental hospital in America (Mexico) 1556
mental hospital in the U.S. (Williamsburg, Virginia) 1773
psychophysicist, Ernst Heinrich Weber 1834
Association of Medical Superintendents of American Institutions for the Insane established 1844
systematically study individual differences (Galton) c. 1869
psychology laboratory founded (by Wilhelm Wundt) 1879
psychology laboratory in the United States (G. Stanley Hall) 1881
psychology book published in America, by John Dewey 1886
American Psychological Association founded 1892
first book on psychoanalysis, *Studies on Hysteria*, by Freud and Breuer, published 1895
American psychiatric institute founded (New York City) 1896
psychiatric ward in an American general hospital established (Albany) 1901
intelligence test (Binet & Simon) 1904
American intelligence test (Stanford-Binet) 1916
mental hygiene international congress held 1930

301. Nonsense Syllables for Learning Experiments

BAZ	MIB	POB
NOC	SOZ	FIW
DIH	HUW	REJ
ZIR	BAX	NIW
PIW	PAZ	WEM
KOG	GIK	ZON
LIR	BUV	LOS
VIT	WUB	LIX
ROX	FUP	ZUF
LIG	PIV	JOL
TIY	FOS	KIF
PUH	SEF	RIW
KOL	POF	JIK
SIM	LOZ	SIF
ZEL	KOD	WIR

302. Five-Letter Anagrams

S T R T U	S R I E F
E S R O C	I C J E U
P T N L A	W T E I H
O I E N S	K K N U S
R O B D A	K C R T A
E P A L P	O M B R O
S T I R W	V R S E E
E L N G A	B Z R A E
T N I A R	S T A T O
S E T N O	L S U K L
Y E L A R	C O N E A
A S T R I	A D R A R
F T I U R	H T M U O
E P N O H	U O F L R
O O C R L	U T T R H
W B N O R	P E S L E
E O C N A	P R U E S
S H U O E	R O T A C
H S E O R	E R G E N
C E L N U	S T A P A
V R P E O	N E P U R
E E S R A	R T A X E
V R E D I	V R B E A
T R O O M	E W R K C
A C E D N	D C U O L
N C O W L	S A S R G

303. Four-Letter Anagrams

N V E O	T W I A
R N O B	E L G U
N E H A	O B N R
S K E D	A T U N
K W L A	S N I K
S N O E	N Z E O
R H I A	I S M W
K I E H	P D N O
K C S O	X I T A
G H H I	M E D O
H C O E	N O C R
T U O A	L D A O
T B A H	I D L O
K O B O	S H D I
T I H C	A L G O
L B L I	S E T R
T O V E	L B A L
T X E I	E N I M
V L E O	M B O C
P C H A	R T N U
O R H E	V D E O
E B U L	P E G A
U R O F	O D F O
Y B B A	T M B O
G F O L	S K I C
R K O F	L P L I
O N N O	I E M C
T D E A	E R T E
E I A D	O A B T
P N A L	R A L O

304. Items for Creativity Brainstorming

Brainstorm creative uses for a:
baseball bat
cane fishing pole
cardboard tube from paper towels
chalkboard eraser
claw hammer
colander
deck of cards
discarded Christmas trees
fruitcake
horseshoe
ice cube tray
jump rope
Manhattan telephone book
megaphone
newspaper
nylon stockings
old shoes
paper clip
pencil
pie pan
plastic milk jug
railroad spike
school bus
shovel
socks with holes in them
soft drink can
square yard of carpet
styrofoam egg carton
thousand ping pong balls
volleyball
used auto tires

305. Self-Help Groups

Abused Women's Aid in Crisis (AWAIC)
Adoptee's Liberty Movement Association
Al-Anon
Alateen
Alcoholics Anonymous (AA)
American Diabetes Association
Arthritis Foundation
Batterers Anonymous
Brain Tumor Support Group
Breathing Partners
Burns Recovered
Calix Society
Candlelighters
Co-dependents Anonymous
Compassionate Friends, The
Debtors Anonymous
Down's Syndrome Congress
Emotions Anonymous
Epilepsy Foundation
Families Anonymous
Gam-Anon
Gamblers Anonymous
Gray Panthers
Heart to Heart
Hospice
International Parents' Organization
Juvenile Diabetes Foundation
Lupus Foundation of America
Make Today Count
Mended Hearts
Mensa

Mothers of Twins Club
Muscular Dystrophy Association
Narcotics Anonymous
National Anorexic Aid Society
National Association for
   Retarded Citizens
National Ataxia Foundation
National Federation of the
   Blind
National Hemophilia Foundation
National Multiple Sclerosis
   Society
National Society for Autistic
   Children
Neurotics Anonymous
Overeaters Anonymous
Paralyzed Veterans of America
Parents and Friends of
   Lesbians and Gays
Parents Anonymous
Parents Without Partners
Reach to Recovery
Recovery, Inc.
Spina Bifida Association
Stroke Clubs
Take Off Pounds Sensibly
   (TOPS)
Theos Foundation
Tourette-Syndrome Association
United Cerebral Palsy
United Ostomy Association
Widowed Persons
Women for Sobriety
Women Who Love Too Much

306. Feelings

adequate
afraid
agitated
alarmed
ambitious
amused
angry
anguished
annoyed
anxious
apathetic
appalled
apprehensive
appreciated
assertive
bad
baffled
befuddled
bold
bored
bothered
brave
bubbly
burdened
calm
capable
caring
cheerful
compassionate
confident

confused
content
courageous
critical
cross
deflated
dejected
delighted
depressed
desperate
despondent
determined
disappointed
disconcerted
disconsolate
disenchanted
disgruntled
disgusted
dismayed
disoriented
displeased
distracted
distraught
distressed
distrustful
disturbed
doubtful
down
downtrodden
ecstatic

elated
empathetic
enduring
energetic
enthralled
envious
euphoric
excited
exasperated
exhausted
exuberant
fearful
fed up
fine
firm
flabbergasted
flustered
forceful
fortunate
fragile
frantic
frightened
frustrated
fulfilled
furious
gay
gentile
glad
gleeful
gloomy
glum
good
great
grieved
happy
hateful
healthy
helpless
hopeless
horrified
hostile
hurt
ill
inadequate
incapable
independent
indestructible
indignant
ineffective
infuriated

intense
intimidated
invisible
irate
irked
irritated
jealous
jolly
jovial
joyful
jubilant
jumpy
left out
leery
lonely
lost
loved
loving
low
lucky
mad
marvelous
mean
melancholy
merry
miserable
mixed up
moody
mournful
motherly
negative
needed
nervous
overjoyed
out of it
outraged
panicky
peaceful
perplexed
persecuted
pleasant
pleased
positive
powerless
proud
relieved
remorseful
resentful
resistant
revengeful

run down
sad
satisfied
secure
serene
serious
somber
sore
sorrowful
sorry
spiteful
spirited
strong
stunned
surprised
terrible
terrified
thankful
thrilled
tickled
timid
tormented
tranquil
trapped
troubled
turned off
uncomfortable
uneasy
unloved
unsure
unwanted
up
uplifted
upset
useless
vibrant
vulnerable
weak
wonderful
worn out
worried

307. The Most Common Fears

speaking before a group
not having enough money
insects and bugs
heights
sickness
dogs
dying
flying
loneliness
deep water
failing
making mistakes
losing friends
looking foolish
tests
bodily injury

308. Commonly Abused Drugs

Name	Street Name
alcohol	booze
amphetamines	speed, uppers
barbiturates	ludes, yellow jackets, reds
cocaine	coke, toot, snow, crack
hashish	herb
heroin	smack, junk, skag
inhalants; aerosols	cans
LSD	acid, dots
MDMA	ecstasy
marijuana	grass, ganja, acapulco
mescaline	cactus
peyote	buttons
psilocybin	magic mushrooms
phencyclidine (PCP)	angel dust

309. Risks of Chronic Alcohol Use

alcohol induced depression
anxiety
birth defects in offspring
blood clotting problems
brain damage
cancer, especially esophagus and stomach
chronic gastritis
cirrhosis of the liver
decreased red blood cell formation
delirium tremens (DT's)
fetal alcohol syndrome
heart disease
inflammation of the pancreas
inflammation of the stomach lining
lower disease resistance
lowered REM sleep
heart muscle tissue damage
memory loss
premature aging syndrome
shorter lifespan (average: 15 years less)

310. Growth Changes of Puberty

Boys	Girls
acne	acne
beard	breast development
chest hair	enlargement of genitals
enlargement of genitals	menstruation
pubic hair	pubic hair
underarm hair	rounding of body shape
voice change	underarm hair

311. Substance Abuse Resources

National Hotlines:

Organization	Phone
Cocaine Helpline	1-800-COCAINE
National Council on Alcoholism	1-800-662-2255
National Federation of Parents for Drug-Free Youth	1-800-554-KIDS
National Institute on Drug Abuse Information and Referral Line	1-800-662-HELP
National Institute on Drug Abuse, Abuse Workplace Helpline	1-800-843-4971
Parents Resource Institute for Drug Educaton (PRIDE)	1-800-241-9746

Information Sources:

American Council for Drug Education
5820 Hubbard Dr.
Rockville, MD 20852

*American Medical Society on Alcoholism
and Other Drug Dependencies*
12 West 12th Street
New York, NY 10010

Committees of Correspondence
57 Conant St., Room 113
Danvers, MA 01923

Do It Now Foundation
P.O. Box 5115, 2050 East University Dr.
Phoenix, AZ 85010

Drug and Alcohol Council
396 Alexander St.
Rochester, NY 14607

Drug Enforcement Administration
1405 I St., NW
Washington, DC 20537

Drugs Anonymous
P.O. Box 473, Ansonia Station
New York, NY 10023

Families Anonymous
P. O. Box 528
14617 Victory Blvd.
Van Nuys, CA 91408

Families in Action
3845 N. Druid Hills Road, Suite 300
Decatur, GA 30033

Hazelden Foundation
P.O. Box 11
Center City, MN 55012

*International Commission for the
Prevention of Alcoholism and Drug
Dependency,* 6830 Laurel St., NW
Washington, DC 20012

Narcotics Anonymous
P.O. Box 9999
Van Nuys, CA 91409

Narcotics Education, Inc.
6830 Laurel St., NW
Washington, DC 20012

*National Association of Alcoholism
and Drug Abuse Counselors*
951 South George Mason Dr.
Arlington, VA 22204

*National Association of Drug
Abuse Problems*
355 Lexington Ave.
New York, NY 10017

*National Clearinghouse for Alcohol
and Drug Information*
P.O. Box 2345
Rockville, MD 20852

National Drug Institute
112 Sladen St.
Dracut, MA 01826

*National Federation of Parents for
Drug-Free Youth*
8730 Georgia Ave., Suite 200
Silver Spring, MD 20910

National Institute on Drug Abuse
Office of Science
5600 Fishers Lane
Rockville, MD 20857

311. Substance Abuse Resources, continued

*National Parent Resource Institute
for Drug Education*
100 Edgewood Ave., Suite 1216
Atlanta, GA 30303

*Parent Resources Institute on Drug
Education*
100 Edgewood Ave., Suite 1216
Atlanta, GA 30303

PharmChem
3925 Bohannon Drive
Menlo Park, CA 94025

Phoenix House
164 W. 7th St.
New York, NY 10023

Pills Anonymous
P.O. Box 473, Ansonia Station
New York, NY 10023

Potsmokers Anonymous
316 East Third St.
New York, NY 10009

312. Common Superstitions

Bad luck to:

walk under a ladder

let a black cat cross your path

sing carols before Christmas season

hang a calendar before January 1

lose a water bucket at sea

see the wedding dress by candlelight

halt a funeral procession

if the bride and groom see each other on their wedding day before the wedding

start a trip on a Friday, especially the 13th

give a person a gift of a knife unless you include a coin

spill ink

spill salt

burn a peach tree

open an umbrella indoors

light three cigarettes on one match

break a mirror

meet on the stairs

turn a feather bed on Sunday

cross knives at the table

enter a house with the left foot first

plant seeds the last three days of March

kill a sparrow

Good luck to:

put money in a wallet given as a gift

carry a silver dollar

wear one's hat backwards

be followed by a strange dog

throw rice at weddings

rub a rabbit's foot

hang a horseshoe on your wall

find a four-leaf clover

receive a coin with a hole in it

wear "something borrowed, something blue, something given, and something new"

be the seventh child

eat cabbage on New Year's day

Predictions

Dropping a knife or fork on the floor foretells a visitor.

A howling dog predicts a death.

A falling window sash or a dog howling at night foretells a death.

Two spoons in one saucer predict a wedding.

Bubbles on tea foretell a kiss is coming.

Cutting hair or nails in a calm at sea will bring rough weather.

Children who play with mirrors become vain.

If your right ear tingles, someone is saying good things about you.

If your left ear tingles, someone is speaking ill of you.

Washing your hands in water in which eggs were boiled will bring you warts.

Eating both ends of a loaf of bread before eating the middle will predict difficulty managing finances.

Smelling flowers growing on a grave may destroy one's sense of smell.

313. Common Nonverbal Gestures

ankles crossed
applause
clasped hands
crossed arms
crossing fingers
crying
eye contact
eyes fluttering
folded arms
frown
genuflection
hands on hips
head in hands
head nods
leaning forward
legs crossed
"OK" sign
raised eyebrows
"raspberries"
rubbing back of
  neck
rubbing bridge
  of nose
rubbing fore-
  head
rubbing hands
  together
scratching head
shoulder shrug
sigh
skipping
smile
steepling hands
sticking tongue out
thumbs up/down
"V" sign
waving
wink
yawn

314. The Endocrine System

adrenal glands
pancreas
parathyroid
pineal gland
pituitary gland
reproductive glands
thyroid gland

315. Parts of the Brain

forebrain:
  telencephalon
    –cerebrum
    –basal
    –corpus callosum
  diencephalon
    –thalamus
    –hypothalamus
midbrain:
  interior colliculi
  superior colliculi
hindbrain:
  cerebellum
  pons
  medulla

316. Right Brain—Left Brain Thinking Modes

Right	Left
nonverbal	verbal
non-rational	rational
concrete	symbolic
holistic	linear
intuitive	logical
better at remembering faces	better at remembering names
expresses feelings	tends to hold on to feelings
short attention span	good ability to concentrate
risk taker	less likely to take risks
likes to draw	likes to read
not concerned with details	likes structure
impulsive	organized
difficulty meeting deadlines	punctual, time conscious
may be messy	neat and tidy

317. Sample Decibel Levels

200	Saturn rocket at close range
150	jet airplane taking off
140	threshold of pain
130	pneumatic hammer
120	rock music amplifiers (5 feet), thunder
110	power mower, riveter
100	circular saw
90	Niagara Falls, vacuum cleaner, subway train
80	truck engine, telephone ringing
70	automobile
60	normal conversation
50	
40	
30	bedroom at night
20	whisper
10	threshold of hearing

318. Forms of Propaganda

appeals to prejudice
glittering generalities
jumping on the bandwagon
name calling
personal testimony
plain folks
stacking the deck
straw man

319. Sentence Stems for Debriefing Experiential Activities

I confirmed . . .	I realized . . .
I discovered . . .	I recognized . . .
I felt . . .	I was surprised . . .
I reinforced . . .	I wonder . . .
I was puzzled . . .	I was disappointed . . .
I learned . . .	I relearned . . .
I reaffirmed . . .	I was pleased . . .

320. Symptoms of Major Depression

sleep disturbance (insomnia, sleeping too much)
crying
"empty" feeling
loss of interest in usually enjoyable activities
difficulty in thinking clearly
feelings of guilt or worthlessness
loss of concentration
lowered self-esteem
not as talkative as usual
excessive fatigue
prolonged sadness
loss of appetite
socially withdrawn
persistent pessimism
significant weight loss
irritability
persistent thoughts of death or suicide
attempted suicide

321. Major Stressors for Adolescents

being in automobile accident
beginning a part-time job
birth of a brother/sister
break-up of relationship
change in dating habits
conflict with a teacher
death of a loved one
divorce of parents
excessively high expectations
failing a test
failing a course
family financial difficulties
fight
fired from a job

illness of family member
illness or injury of a friend
low grades
moving
peer pressure
personal injury
pregnancy
rejection of a peer
major illness
separation of parents
taking a vacation
traffic ticket
transferring to a new school

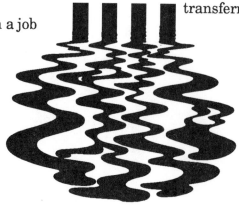

322. Physical Symptoms of Stress

acne
accelerated heart
  rate
asthma attack
backaches
blushing
cold hands
colds
constipation
diarrhea
dilated pupils
dry mouth
exhaustion
fainting
fatigue
erratic heart beat

hands shaking
headaches
higher blood pressure
hunger
muscle pain
nausea
neck aches
nervousness
perspiration
sexual dysfunction
shortness of breath
skin rash
sleep disturbance
sweaty palms
trembling
upset stomach

323. Mental Symptoms of Stress

critical of others
decreased creativity
denial
diminished fantasy life
forgetfulness
helplessness
impaired concentration
impatience
indecisiveness
inflexibility
loss of confidence
loss of objectivity
loss of sense of humor
lowered self-esteem

overplanning
pessimism
poor decision making
preoccupation
problem avoidance
sarcasm
self-defeating thoughts
selfishness
self-pity
sense of urgency
stubbornness
short temper

324. Emotional Symptoms of Stress

alarmed
anger
anxiety
apprehension
burdened
depression
dread
fear
frustration
grief
guilt

hopelessness
inadequacy
irritability
moodiness
panic
resentment
restlessness
tension
terror
worry

325. Behavioral Responses to Stress

absenteeism
acting out
aggression
alcohol abuse
arguing
behavioral tics
change in sleep patterns
change of work habits
clenching one's jaw
compulsive behaviors
crying
drug abuse
excessive eating
excessive risk taking
excessive chatter
fidgeting
fighting
grinding teeth in sleep
hitting

nail biting
pacing
nervous laughter
ritualistic behaviors
screaming
self-indulgence
shifty eyes
shopping
sighing
smoking
staring into space
stuttering
tantrums
throwing things
voice tone change
using obscenities
withdrawing
working

326. Stress Prevention Techniques

avoid catastrophizing
avoid getting too wrapped up in
 yourself
avoid overcommitment
avoid perfectionism
avoid putting yourself down
avoid unnecessary arguments
be an actor, not a reactor
be prepared
be thankful
choose to be happy
clarify the expectations of others
clarify your expectations
cultivate new relationships
decorate your environment
develop a support network
develop self-affirming habits
distinguish between needs and wants
do one thing at a time
eliminate a self-defeating behavior
eat a healthy diet
eliminate needless worry
find some time to be alone
forgive
get adequate rest
get organized
get up 10 minutes earlier
have a good belly laugh

have a pet
help others
keep a balance in your activities
keep a journal
know and accept yourself
learn responsible assertiveness
learn to say "no"
list your strengths and successes
maintain a sense of humor
make effective planning a habit
monitor your stress level
reexamine your "shoulds" and
 "musts"
regular exercise
remember to play
set long-range goals
set priorities
smile
stop to smell the roses
strive for an open mind
sufficient sleep
supportive relationships
take time to relax
treat others with kindness
try to remain flexible
unclutter your life
volunteer for a worthy cause

327. Stress Reduction Techniques

aerobic exercise
apologize
ask someone for help
biofeedback
challenge your assumptions
challenge your irrational self-talk
counseling
cry
dancing
engage in a hobby
hug someone
join a self-help group
just listen
keep things in perspective
listening to favorite music
make a list
massage
meditation
never make important
  decisions after midnight
play a musical instrument
problem solve
progressive relaxation
read
recall a pleasant experience
relax your jaw
remember that tomorrow is a
  new day

seek a different perspective
self-affirmation
singing
stretch
take a break
take a warm bath
take a nap
take a walk
take three slow, deep breaths
talk with someone you trust
visualize a calming scene
write a letter

328. Time Management Strategies

Know your goals. What do you want to accomplish?

Set priorities.

Handle each piece of paper once.

Think through a job before starting.

Make a list of points to discuss before telephoning.

Have an organized filing system.

Finish one task before beginning another.

Group routine and trivial tasks.

Practice increasing reading speed.

Listen carefully.

Do the most important things first.

Throw away all the paper you can.

Keep an orderly desk and room.

Maintain a "TO DO" list.

Consolidate shopping and errands.

Terminate non-productive activities as soon as possible.

Don't dwell on the past.

Guard your physical health with sufficient sleep and exercise.

Allow flexibility in your schedule for unexpected events.

Set deadlines for yourself.

Break major goals into subgoals.

Anticipate disruptions; have a backup plan.

Keep a calendar of important events.

Don't abuse the time of others.

Allow enough time for planning.

Fix a starting and finishing time for each project.

Develop an idea notebook.

Be selective in television viewing.

Reward yourself for completion of projects.

Work smarter, not harder.

Keep a time log to see how you are using your time.

Minimize interruptions when studying.

Recognize when you are procrastinating.

Eliminate tasks which do not contribute to your goals.

Set aside quiet think time.

Take occasional short breaks.

Put waiting time to good use; read or work on small tasks.

Do least enjoyable chores first.

Use your wastebasket freely.

Learn to say "no."

Plan as far ahead as possible.

Break big jobs into smaller tasks.

Have a place for everything.

Examine old habits for time wasters.

Eat a light lunch to avoid afternoon drowsiness.

Don't mistake activity for productivity.

Maintain a balance between work, school, and leisure activities.

Discover your most creative time of day.

Keep a notepad by your bed.

Combine tasks whenever possible.

Develop checklists in planning.

Designate a specific place where you place all items to be taken to school with you the next day.

Take sufficient time to carefully weigh important decisions.

Know thyself. Be aware of your strengths and limitations.

Periodically evaluate the progress toward your goals.

Do one thing at a time.

Don't rely upon your memory for important events, ideas, or dates. Write them down on your calendar or notebook.

Don't dwell on unimportant decisions.

329. Effective Study Strategies

Read the text assignments before going to class.

Sit in the front of the classroom.

Write down clear directions for all assignments.

Focus on *what* the teacher is saying, not how.

Scan reading materials before reading.

Type papers when possible.

Develop mnemonics when possible.

Keep a calendar of major events including tests, deadlines, etc.

Set up a study area for that purpose only.

Work on one assignment at a time.

Keep all the supplies and materials you need readily available.

Take periodic breaks (5-10 minutes each hour).

Underline major points in your notes.

Get together study groups to review before tests.

Pay special attention to the first and last five minutes of the class.

Ask questions if you don't understand.

Several shorter study periods are better than one long one.

Break large assignments into a number of smaller tasks.

Get a good night's rest before an exam.

Read through the entire exam before beginning.

Answer the easiest questions first.

Pace yourself to allow adequate time for each question.

Use five-minute blocks of free time to review notes.

330. Self-Discovery Sentence Stems

One thing I do well is . . .
My greatest peeve is . . .
One thing I would like to do
 better is . . .
I enjoy . . .
Success in life is . . .
If I were rich I would . . .
I value . . .
I am deeply concerned about . . .
I would most like to improve . . .
I want to . . .
Probably my strongest asset
 is . . .
I work best when . . .
People are . . .
When I don't get my way I . . .
I am happiest when . . .
I wish my parents would . . .
I am sad when . . .
If I were 21 I would . . .
I resent . . .
I wish I had . . .
I feel important when . . .
I believe . . .
My favorite teacher . . .
I worry about . . .
People would be happier if
 they . . .
Most people treat me . . .
Someday I expect to . . .
If I had one wish it would
 be . . .
I suffer most from . . .
If I were president, I
 would . . .
I am . . .
My greatest ambition is . . .
My favorite place is . . .
I become angry when . . .
I am scared when . . .
I feel uncomfortable when . . .
I hope to . . .
I think I am . . .

I know I can . . .
I am not afraid to . . .
A true leader is . . .
I admire people who . . .
I sometimes wonder . . .
I would like to learn . . .
One risk I took was . . .
I am probably too . . .
My body is . . .
For me, school has usually been . . .
The high point of my week was . . .
A good friend will . . .
Next year I hope to . . .
The best teachers are the ones
 who . . .
I want to be remembered as . . .
I like people who . . .
Religion is . . .
I wish I knew how to . . .
I'd like to change . . .
I enjoy being with . . .
Happiness is . . .
It is unfair that . . .
I get down in the dumps when . . .
I plan to . . .
I appreciate my parents for . . .
I find it easy to . . .
It is difficult for me to . . .
Most people think I am . . .
Most people would be surprised to
 know that I . . .
The most frustrating thing for me
 is . . .
Teachers usually treat me . . .
If people only knew . . .
Our school needs . . .

331. Self-Discovery Questions

What do you enjoy most?
Who are you?
What do you hope to be doing in five years?
What makes you happy?
What do you do well?
What is the best thing that could happen to you?
How would you like to be remembered?
What would you like to change in your life?
How do you deal with anger?
Do you have any dreams?
Whom do you admire most?
What is your biggest peeve?
What three words would you most want others to use in describing you?
When do you like yourself best?
How do you have fun?
How would you define success?
What would you like to tell your teacher?
What would you like to learn that they haven't taught you in school?

332. Life Goals

Aid my favorite charity
Be a community leader
Be a public speaker
Be in a play
Be more assertive
Become a good conversationalist
Become a millionaire
Become more positive
Build my dream house
Climb a mountain
Cultivate a flower garden
Earn a college degree
Gain public distinction
Get married
Help those less fortunate
Improve family relationships
Learn to fly an airplane
Learn to play a musical instrument
Learn to relax
Live a long life
Lose weight
Make new friends

Manage time better
Move to different climate
Own a special car
Own my own business
Participate in professional sports
Play in a rock band
Quit smoking
Raise a large family
Retire financially secure
Run a marathon
Star in a movie
Start my own business
Travel
Win a beauty contest
Work to spread my religion
Write a book

333. Hearing Impaired Persons of Note

Jack Ashley	1922-	member of British Parliament
Ludwig van Beethoven	1770-1827	composer
Linda Bove	1945-	*Sesame Street* actress
John Brewster, Jr.	1766-1854	American artist
John Carlin	1813-1891	artist, poet
John Louis Clark	1881-1970	wood sculptor
John W. Cornforth	1917-	Nobel chemist
Rolando Lopez Dirube	1928-	Cuban artist
Thomas Alva Edison	1847-1931	inventor
Nanette Fabray	1920-	actress
Phyllis Frelich	1944-	actress
Antonio Feu Gómez	1907-1984	Spanish artist
John Goodricke	1764-1786	astronomer
Francisco Goya	1746-1828	Spanish artist
John R. Gregg	1867-1948	short-hand inventor
Olof Hanson	1862-1933	architect
William Hoy	1862-1961	major league baseball player
George Hyde	1882-1968	historian
Jack Jones	1923-1983	cultural historian
Helen Keller	1880-1968	author, lecturer
John Kitto	1804-1854	Bible scholar
Judith G. Low	1860-1927	founded Girl Scouts of America
René Princeteau	1843-1914	French painter
Ronald Reagan	1911-	U.S. President
Laura Searing	1840-1923	journalist
Erastus Smith	1787-1837	scout for Sam Houston
Alfred Thomson	1894-1979	artist
Douglas Tilden	1860-1935	sculptor
Cadwallader Washburn	1866-1965	artist
Peter Wolf	1945-	TV, film director
Frances Woods	1907-	dancer
David Wright	1920-	poet

334. Psychoses and Neuroses in Fiction

Bartleby the Scrivener, Herman Melville
The Black Wedding, Isaac Singer
The Crack-Up, F. Scott Fitzgerald
Diary of a Madman, Nicolai Gogol
The End of the Party, Graham Greene
The Eternal Husband, Fyodor Dostoevsky
Flotsam and Jetsam, W. Somerset Maugham
Hamlet, William Shakespeare
He? Guy de Maupassant
Home of the Brave, Arthur Laurents
Jordi, Theodore Isaac Rubin
The Judgment, Franz Kafka
Louis Lambert, Honoré Balzac
The Lost Phoebe, Theodore Dreiser
Macbeth, William Shakespeare
Madam Bovary, Gustave Flaubert
One Flew Over the Cuckoo's Nest, Ken Kesey
Pigeon Feathers, John Updike
The Room, Jean Paul Sartre
Tender Is the Night, F. Scott Fitzgerald
The Vagabond, Collette
The Yellow Wallpaper, Charlotte Perkins Gilman
Waiting for Godot, Samuel Beckett
Ward No. 6, Anton Chekhov

335. Common Personality Characteristics

absent-minded
affectionate
aggressive
aloof
altruistic
ambitious
anxious
assertive
bossy
calm
candid
cautious
charming
cheerful
clever
cocky
compassionate
competitive
compulsive
confident
conforming
cooperative
critical
defensive
dependable
dependent
determined
dishonest
disorderly
dominant
dull
energetic
excitable
exuberant
feminine
fickle
flexible
friendly
frivolous
funny
generous
good-natured
gregarious
happy
helpless

honest
hostile
humane
humble
humorous
imaginative
impulsive
indecisive
independent
indifferent
intolerant
irritable
jealous
jovial
kind
lazy
liberal
miserly
moralistic
optimistic
outgoing
overbearing
passionate
persistent
pessimistic
placid
pleasant
poised
polite
popular
practical
proper
pushy
reasonable
rebellious
reliable
reserved
restless
rude
sadistic
sarcastic
self-centered
selfish
sensitive
sentimental

serious
shrewd
shy
sincere
sly
sociable
sophisticated
strong
stubborn
studious
suspicious
sympathetic
tactless
temperamental
tense
timid
tolerant
understanding
uninhibited
unreliable
unstable
versatile
vibrant
warm
weak
wise

336. Psychology Related Journals

Adolescence
American Journal of
    Orthopsychiatry
American Journal of Drug and
    Alcohol Abuse
American Journal of Psychology
American Psychologist
Child Development
Contemporary Psychology
Counseling and Development
    Journal
Developmental Psychology
Family Therapy
Gerontologist
Journal of Abnormal Psychology
Journal of Applied Behavioral
    Analysis
Journal of Applied Psychology
Journal of Community Psychology
Journal of Comparative and
    Physiological Psychology
Journal of Contemporary Psycho-
    therapy
Journal of Counseling Psychology
Journal of Creative Behavior
Journal of Cross-Cultural
    Psychology
Journal of Educational Psychology
Journal of Emotional Education
Journal of the Experimental Analysis of Behavior
Journal of Experimental Psychology
Journal of Experimental Child Psychology
Journal of General Psychology

Journal of History of the
    Behavioral Sciences
Journal of Humanistic Psychology
Journal of Individual Psychology
Journal of Offender Counseling,
    Services and Rehabilitation
Journal of Personality
Journal of Personality and
    Social Psychology
Journal of Psychology
Journal of Social Issues
Journal of Social Psychology
Journal of Transpersonal Psychology
Journal of Vocational Behavior
Journal of Youth and Adolescence
Perceptual and Motor Skills
Psychological Record
Psychological Reports
Psychological Research
Psychological Review
Psychology in the Schools
Psychology Today
Rehabilitation Psychology
Scientific American
Small Group Behavior
Youth and Society

Section VII

LISTS FOR GEOGRAPHY

337. Current Names of Old Places

Current Name	Old Name	Current Name	Old Name
Bangladesh	East Pakistan	Namibia	South West Africa
Beijing	Peking; Peiping	Naples, Italy	Neapolis
Belize	British Honduras	New York City	New Amsterdam
Benin	Dahomey	Oslo	Christiania
Botswana	Bechuanaland	Paris	Lutetia Parisiorium
Casablanca	Anfa	Pittsburgh	Fort Dusquene
Central African Republic	Ubangi-Shari	Pyongyan, North Korea	Heijo
Cologne	Colonia Agrippa	Salvador	Bahia
Detroit	Fort Lernoult	Seoul, South Korea	Keijo
Donesk, USSR	Stalino		
Ethiopia	Abyssinia	Shanghai, China	Hu-tsen
France	Gaul	Shenyang, China	Mukden
Gdansk	Danzig	Singapore	Singhapura
Ghana	Gold Coast	Sofia, Bulgaria	Sardica
Gorky, USSR	Nizhni Novgorod	Sri Lanka	Celyon
Ho Chi Minh City	Saigon	Sudan	Nubia
Hyderabad, India	Golconda	Sverdlovsk, USSR	Ekaterinburg
Indonesia	Netherlands East Indies	Thailand	Siam
		Tanzania	German East Africa
Iran	Persia	Tokyo	Edo
Iraq	Mesopotamia	Toronto	Fort Rouille; York
Istanbul	Constantinople; Byzantium	Tripoli, Libya	Oea
		Turin, Italy	Augusta Taurinorum
Kinshasa, Zaire	Leopoldville	Turkey	Ottoman Empire
St. Petersburg	Leningrad	Vancouver, Canada	Granville
Lesotho	Basutoland		
London	Londinium	Vietnam	Indochina
Malagasy Republic	Madagascar	Volgograd	Stalingrad; Tsaritsyn
Malawi	Nyasaland	Zaire	Congo
Marseilles, France	Massilia	Zimbabwe	Rhodesia
Mexico City	Tenochtitlan		

338. Types of Maps

atlas
aeronautical chart
celestial globe
globe
political map
physical map
relief map
road map
survey maps
terrain map
terrestrial globe
transportation map
weather map

339. Map Features

equator
graphic scale
grid lines
index
isolines
latitude
longitude
Mercator projection
meridians
parallels
projection
scale
symbols

340. Topographical Features

bays	islands
beaches	jungles
canals	lakes
canyons	mountains
caves	oceans
cities	plains
dams	ravines
deltas	rivers
deserts	roads
dunes	savannas
fjords	shoals
floodplains	streams
forests	swamps
glaciers	tundra
gorges	tunnels
grasslands	valleys
hills	waterfalls

341. The Continents

Continents	Square miles
Asia	17,226,000
Africa	11,667,000
Antarctica	5,500,000
Australia	3,000,000
Europe	4,056,000
North America	9,355,000
South America	6,878,000

342. The Seas and Oceans

Andaman Sea	Indian Ocean
Arctic Ocean	Mediterranean Sea
Atlantic Ocean	North Sea
Baltic Sea	Pacific Ocean
Bering Sea	Persian Gulf
Black Sea	Red Sea
Caribbean Sea	Sea of Japan
East China Sea	Sea of Okhotsk
Gulf of Mexico	South China Sea
Hudson Bay	Yellow Sea

343. States and Their Capitals

State	Capital	State	Capital
Alabama	Montgomery	Montana	Helena
Alaska	Juneau	Nebraska	Lincoln
Arizona	Phoenix	Nevada	Carson City
Arkansas	Little Rock	New Hampshire	Concord
California	Sacramento	New Jersey	Trenton
Colorado	Denver	New Mexico	Santa Fe
Connecticut	Hartford	New York	Albany
Delaware	Dover	North Carolina	Raleigh
Florida	Tallahassee	North Dakota	Bismarck
Georgia	Atlanta	Ohio	Columbus
Hawaii	Honolulu	Oklahoma	Oklahoma City
Idaho	Boise	Oregon	Salem
Illinois	Springfield	Pennsylvania	Harrisburg
Indiana	Indianapolis	Rhode Island	Providence
Iowa	Des Moines	South Carolina	Columbia
Kansas	Topeka	South Dakota	Pierre
Kentucky	Frankfort	Tennessee	Nashville
Louisiana	Baton Rouge	Texas	Austin
Maine	Augusta	Utah	Salt Lake City
Maryland	Annapolis	Vermont	Montpelier
Massachusetts	Boston	Virginia	Richmond
Michigan	Lansing	Washington	Olympia
Minnesota	St. Paul	West Virginia	Charleston
Mississippi	Jackson	Wisconsin	Madison
Missouri	Jefferson City	Wyoming	Cheyenne

344. Abbreviations of the States

Alabama	AL	Montana	MT
Alaska	AK	Nebraska	NE
Arizona	AZ	Nevada	NV
Arkansas	AR	New Hampshire	NH
California	CA	New Jersey	NJ
Colorado	CO	New Mexico	NM
Connecticut	CT	New York	NY
Delaware	DE	North Carolina	NC
Florida	FL	North Dakota	ND
Georgia	GA	Ohio	OH
Hawaii	HI	Oklahoma	OK
Idaho	ID	Oregon	OR
Illinois	IL	Pennsylvania	PA
Indiana	IN	Rhode Island	RI
Iowa	IA	South Carolina	SC
Kansas	KS	South Dakota	SD
Kentucky	KY	Tennessee	TN
Louisiana	LA	Texas	TX
Maine	ME	Utah	UT
Maryland	MD	Vermont	VT
Massachusetts	MA	Virginia	VA
Michigan	MI	Washington	WA
Minnesota	MN	West Virginia	WV
Mississippi	MS	Wisconsin	WI
Missouri	MO	Wyoming	WY

345. Nicknames of the States

Alabama	Heart of Dixie; Yellowhammer State; Camellia State
Alaska	Land of the Midnight Sun; The Last Frontier
Arizona	Grand Canyon State; Copper State
Arkansas	Hot Water State; The Land of Opportunity
California	Golden State
Colorado	Centennial State; Highest State
Connecticut	Constitution State; Nutmeg State
Delaware	First State; Diamond State
Florida	Sunshine State; Orange State
Georgia	Peach State; Goober State
Hawaii	Aloha State; Pineapple State
Idaho	Gem State
Illinois	Prairie State; Land of Lincoln
Indiana	Hoosier State
Iowa	Hawkeye State
Kansas	Sunflower State; Jayhawk State
Kentucky	Bluegrass State; Tobacco State
Louisiana	Bayou State; Fisherman's Paradise; Pelican State
Maine	Border State; Pine Tree State
Maryland	Old Line State; The Free State
Massachusetts	Pilgrim State; Bay State
Michigan	Wolverine State; Auto State; Great Lake State
Minnesota	North Star State; Gopher State
Mississippi	Magnolia State; Eagle State
Missouri	Show Me State; Ozark State
Montana	Big Sky Country; Bonanza State; Treasure State
Nebraska	Tree Planter State; Cornhusker State
Nevada	Sage State; Silver State
New Hampshire	Granite State; Mother of Rivers
New Jersey	Garden State; Clam State
New Mexico	Cactus State; Land of Enchantment
New York	Empire State; Knickerbocker State
North Carolina	Old North State; Tarheel State; Terpentine State
North Dakota	Sioux State; Flickertail State; Peace Garden State
Ohio	Buckeye State
Oklahoma	Sooner State
Oregon	Beaver State
Pennsylvania	Keystone State; Quaker State
Rhode Island	Plantation State; Ocean State
South Carolina	Rice State; Swamp State; Iodine State
South Dakota	Sunshine State; Coyote State
Tennessee	Volunteer State
Texas	Lone Star State
Utah	Beehive State
Vermont	Green Mountain State
Virginia	Old Dominion; Cavalier State
Washington	Evergreen State; Chinook State
West Virginia	Mountain State
Wisconsin	Badger State; Copper State
Wyoming	Equality State; Cowboy State

346. Origins of State Names

Alabama	Creek Indian for "place of rest"
Alaska	from Eskimo word *alakshak* which means "peninsula" or "great lands"
Arizona	derived from Indian word for "little place of springs" or from Aztec *arizuma* which means "silver bearing"
Arkansas	from French name for the Ogala Sioux
California	from Spanish *caliento forno* or "hot furance," the name of a fictitious Spanish paradise
Colorado	derived from Spanish word for red
Connecticut	probably from Indian word "Quonoktacut" given the river which ran through that area
Delaware	after Lord De La Warr, the Virginia governor
Florida	from Spanish *Pascua floride* or flowery Easter, named by Ponce de Leon in his 1513 visit
Georgia	named in honor of King George II of England
Hawaii	probably from native word *hawaiki* or "homeland"
Idaho	supposedly from an Indiana word for "light on the hills"
Illinois	from French version of *Illini*, Indian word for men
Indiana	"land of the Indians"
Iowa	possibly from Sioux word meaning "sleepy waters" or "drowsy ones"
Kansas	after the Kansas Indian tribe; meaning "south wind people"
Kentucky	perhaps from the Indian name *Kentake* for "plains" or "meadow lands"
Louisiana	in honor of French King Louis XIV
Maine	from old French word meaning "province"
Maryland	named after Queen Henrietta Maria of England
Massachusetts	from Algonquin word *Massadchu-es-et* meaning great hills
Michigan	from Indian word for "great water"

346. Origins of the State Names, continued

Minnesota	from Sioux word for "cloudy water" or "muddy water" describing the Minnesota River
Mississippi	from Indian word for great river
Missouri	from an Indian tribe whose name meant "muddy stream"
Montana	from Spanish or Latin word for "mountain"
Nebraska	from Omaha Indian word for "broad river" or "shallow river"
Nevada	from Spanish for "snow covered"
New Hampshire	named after Hampshire County, England
New Jersey	named for Isle of Jersey in the English Channel
New Mexico	after the Aztec god, *Mexitl*
New York	in honor of the Duke of York
North Carolina	from Latin word for Charles; in honor of King Charles I
North Dakota	from a Sioux name meaning "ally"
Ohio	from Iroquois word meaning "good river" or "beautiful river"
Oklahoma	from Choctaw Indian word for "red man"
Oregon	uncertain; perhaps from an Indian word meaning "beautiful water"
Pennsylvania	in honor of William Penn, the state's founder
Rhode Island	perhaps from Dutch word for "red clay"
South Carolina	from Latin word for Charles; in honor of King Charles I
South Dakota	from a Sioux name meaning "ally"
Tennessee	from a Cherokee village called *tanasse*
Texas	after the Texas Indian tribe
Utah	named for the Ute Indians
Vermont	probably from French, *vert mont*, or green mountain
Virginia	named for the Virgin Queen of England, Elizabeth I
Washington	in honor of George Washington
West Virginia	carved from Virginia during the Civil War
Wisconsin	from Chippewa word *Miskonsin* meaning "grassy place"
Wyoming	from Indian word for "large prairies"

347. 20 Largest Cities in the United States

New York
Los Angeles
Chicago
Houston
Philadelphia
San Diego
Detroit
Dallas
San Antonio
Phoenix
Baltimore
San Jose
San Francisco
Indianapolis
Memphis
Jacksonville
Washington
Milwaukee
Boston
Columbus

348. Provinces and Territories of Canada

Province	Capital
Alberta	Edmonton
British Columbia	Victoria
Manitoba	Winnipeg
New Brunswick	Fredericton
Newfoundland	St. John's
Nova Scotia	Halifax
Ontario	Toronto
Prince Edward Island	Charlottetown
Quebec	Quebec
Saskatchewan	Regina

Territories	Capital
Northwest Territory	Yellowknife
Yukon Territory	Whitehorse

349. The 20 Most Populous Countries (in millions)

China	1,120
India	888
Soviet Union	290
United States	255
Indonesia	190
Brazil	155
Japan	126
Nigeria	117
Pakistan	115
Bangladesh	114
Mexico	89
Germany	72
Vietnam	69
Italy	58
United Kingdom	58
France	56
Philippines	56
Turkey	56
Thailand	55
Iran	55

350. Longest Rivers

Name	Location
Nile	Africa
Amazon	South America
Yangtze	Asia
Huang Ho	Asia
Congo	Africa
Amur	Asia
Lena	Asia
Irtysh	Asia
Mackenzie	North America
Mekong	Asia
Niger	Africa
Yenisey	Asia
Paraná	South America
Mississippi	North America
Missouri	North America

351. Active Volcanoes in the United States

Volcano	State	Volcano	State
Gareloi	Alaska	Veniaminof	Alaska
Cleveland	Alaska	Redoubt	Alaska
Okmok	Alaska	Kilaues	Hawaii
Akutan	Alaska	Mount St.	Washington
Pavlof	Alaska	Helens	

352. Weather Signs from American Folklore

If crows fly low, winds going to blow.
  Crows fly high, winds going to die.

Red sky in the morning, sailors take warning.
  Red sky at night, sailor's delight.

Onion skins thin, mild winter coming in.
  Onion skins tough, winter will be rough.

When the grass is dry at morning light, look for rain before the night.
  When the dew is on the grass, rain will never come to pass.

When leaves show their undersides,
  Be very sure rain betides.

Thicker corn husks predict a cold winter.

Flies bite more right before a rain.

If the groundhog see his shadow on February 2, there will be six more weeks of winter.

The wider the middle band on the wooly bear, the milder the winter ahead.

When the wind is in the east 'tis neither good for man nor beast.

If the first snowflakes of the storm are large, it will not last long.

If autumn is foggy expect more snow this winter.

High clouds foretell good weather.

Clear moon, frost soon.

If your hair becomes limp rain is near.

A sunshiny shower won't last an hour.

When the smoke descends, good weather ends.

Crickets chirp slower as it gets colder.

Leaves turning inside out precede the onset of rain.

If it is wet on Friday, Saturday, and Sunday, expect it to be wet all week.

Cows or mules or woolyworms growing thick hair foretells a cold winter.

A large crop of walnuts or acorns predicts cold winter.

Dust devils predict bad weather.

Tough apple skins foretell a hard winter.

Bees stay close to their hives when rain is coming.

Swallows fly close to the ground before a rain.

Thick cornshucks mean a bad winter is coming.

If the first of April is foggy, there will be floods in June.

A Saturday rainbow will be followed by a week of rain.

Trees grow dark before a storm.

Northeast winds in winter bring heavy snow.

A hog carrying a stick of wood forebodes bad weather.

A morning rainbow in the western sky suggests rain will be coming.

A year of snow, a year of plenty.

353. Weather Extremes

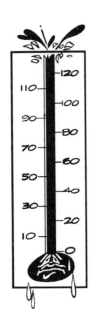

Lowest temperature:	-126.9 degrees F	Antarctica	1960
Highest temperature:	136.4 degrees F	Libya	1922
Lowest rainfall:	.03 in./yr.	Arica, Chile	average
Heaviest rainfall:	73.6 in./24 hrs.	Reunion Island	1952
Strongest winds:	188 mph	New Hampshire	1934
Largest hailstone:	1 pound	Kansas	1970

354. Types of Clouds

altocumulus
altostratus
cirrocumulus
cirrostratus
cirrus
cumulonimbus
cumulus
nimbostratus
stratocumulus
stratus

355. Weather Terms

air mass
barometric pressure
blizzard
breeze
cloud
cloudburst
cyclone
dew point
drought
fog
flood
front
frost
gale
hail
high-pressure area
humidity
hurricane
ice
jet stream

lightning
low-pressure area
monsoon
precipitation
rainbow
rain
sleet
snow
squall
storm
sunshine
temperature
thunder
thunderstorm
tide
tornado
typhoon
waterspout
wind

356. Major Crops of the United States

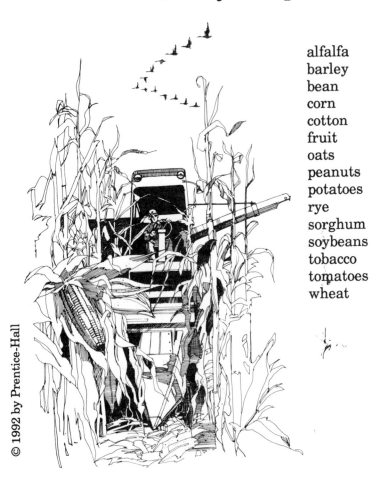

alfalfa
barley
bean
corn
cotton
fruit
oats
peanuts
potatoes
rye
sorghum
soybeans
tobacco
tomatoes
wheat

357. Farm Animals

cattle
chicken
ducks
goats
horses
pigs
rabbits
sheep
turkeys

358. Fields of Geology and Geography

Field	Study of . . .
climatology	patterns of weather
cultural geography	location and spread of cultures
economic geology	geologic materials of use to industry
economic geography	location and distribution of economic activities
environmental geology	solving environmental problems using geological knowledge
geophysics	development and composition of the earth
historical geography	changes and patterns of human activities
human geography	patterns of human activity and interaction with environment
hydrology	distribution and movement of water on the earth
mineralogy	minerals
oceanography	oceans and ocean life forms
petrology	origin, characteristics and structure of rocks
planetology	physical and chemical make-up of the planets
population geography	changes in patterns of population
soil geography	distribution of soils
structural geology	the shapes and positions and movements of rocks deep beneath the earth's surface
geomorphology	the earth's surface and its changes
glacial geology	glaciers and their effect on the earth's surface
sedimentology	sediment and how it is deposited
seismology	earthquakes
paleontology	fossils
urban geography	cities and urban areas
zoogeographers	animal habitats

359. Careers in Geography

cartographer
census planner
cultural geographer
demographer
economic geographer
land-use specialist

park ranger
political geographer
population analyst
teacher
weather forecaster

360. The Great Lakes

Lakes	Maximum Depth (feet)
Erie	210
Huron	750
Michigan	923
Ontario	802
Superior	1,333

361. Largest Lakes

Caspian Sea
Lake Superior
Lake Victoria
Aral Sea
Lake Huron
Lake Michigan
Lake Tanganyika
Great Bear Lake
Lake Baikal
Lake Nyasa

362. Major Deserts

Desert	Location
Atacama	Chile
Gobi	Mongolia
Great Arabian	Middle East
Great Australian	Australia
Kalahari	South Africa
Kara Kum	USSR
Kyzyl Kum	USSR
Libyan	Libya
Mojave	U.S.
Painted Desert	U.S.
Sahara	North Africa
Takla Makan	China
Thar	India-Pakistan

363. Largest Islands

Greenland
New Guinea
Borneo
Madagascar
Baffin
Sumatra
Great Britain
Honshu
Victoria
Ellesmere

364. Tallest Buildings in North America

Building	City	Height (feet)
Sears Tower	Chicago	1,454
World Trade Center	New York City	1,350
Empire State Building	New York City	1,250
Amoco	Chicago	1,136
John Hancock	Chicago	1,127
Texas Commerce Tower	Houston	1,002

The CN Tower in Toronto, Ontario is 1,821 feet tall, making it the world's tallest self-supporting structure.

365. Lowest Spots on Each Continent

Continent	Location	Feet below sea level
Asia	Dead Sea (Israel & Jordan)	1,290
Africa	Quattara Depression (Egypt)	440
Australia	Lake Eyre	39
Europe	Caspian Sea (U.S.S.R.)	96
North America	Death Valley (United States)	282
South America	Salinas Grande (Argentina)	131

366. Types of Volcanoes

Cinder Cones
Composite Volcanoes
Lava Domes
Shield Volcanoes
Submarine Volcanoes

367. Geographic Nicknames

Name	Nickname
Alexandria, Egypt	Mother of Books
Atlantic Ocean	The Herring Pond
Australia	New Holland
Balkans	Powder Keg of Europe
Boston	Bean Town
Chicago	Windy City
Dallas	Big "D"
Denver	Mile High City
Detroit	Motor City
Europe	Old World
Hispania	Spain
Hollywood	Film Capital of the World
Iceland	Land of Frost and Fire
Ireland	Emerald Isle
Italy	Garden of Europe
Kiev	Russian Mother of Cities
Los Angeles	LA; City of the Angels
Mexico	New Spain
Nashville	Music City, U.S.A.
New York City	The Big Apple
Novosibirsk, USSR	Chicago of Siberia
Panama	Crossroads of the World
Paris	City of Light
Philadelphia	Philly; City of Brotherly Love
Pittsburgh	The Steel City
St. Louis	Gateway of the West
San Francisco	Frisco; The Golden Gate City

368. World Currencies

Country	Unit	Equivalent
Afghanistan	afghani	100 puls
Argentina	peso	100 centavos
Australia	dollar	100 cents
Austria	schilling	100 groschen
Belgium	franc	100 centimes
Brazil	cruzeiro	100 centavos
Bulgaria	lev	100 stotinki
Canada	dollar	100 cents
China	yuan	100 fen
Egypt	pound	100 piasters
France	franc	100 centimes
Great Britain	pound	100 pence
Haiti	gourde	100 centimes
India	rupee	100 paisa
Iran	rial	100 dinars
Israel	shekel	100 new agorot
Italy	lira	100 centesimi
Japan	yen	100 sen
Korea	won	100 chun
Mexico	peso	100 centavos
Peru	sol	100 centavos
Poland	zloty	100 groszy
Russia	ruble	100 kopecks
South Africa	rand	100 cents
Spain	peseta	100 centimos
Switzerland	franc	100 centimes
Turkey	lira	100 kurus
United States	dollar	100 cents
Yugoslavia	dinar	100 par

369. Soybean Products

adhesive tape	cooking oil	ice cream	processed meat
baby food	cosmetics	insect sprays	salad dressings
candles	disinfectants	leather softeners	soaps
candy	explosives	linoleum	soy sauce
carbon paper	fertilizer	mayonnaise	textiles
cattle feed	fire extin-	medicines	varnishes
	guisher fluid	paint	

370. Major Wine Producing Countries (in order of production)

Italy
France
Spain
Russia
Argentina
United States
Portugal
Romania
Yugoslavia

371. Major Wheat Producing Countries (in order of production)

Russia
United States
China
India
Canada
France
Australia
Turkey
Pakistan
Italy

372. Major Petroleum Producing Countries (in approximate order of production)

Russia
United States
Saudi Arabia
Mexico
Great Britain
China
Iran
Venezuela
Indonesia
Nigeria

373. Countries and Capitals of South America

Country	Capital
Argentina	Buenos Aires
Bolivia	La Paz; Sucre
Brazil	Brasilia
Chile	Santiago
Columbia	Bogotá
Ecuador	Quito
Guyana	Georgetown
Paraguay	Asunción
Peru	Lima
Surinam	Paramaribo
Uraguay	Montevideo
Venezuela	Caracas

374. Countries and Capitals of North and Central America

Country	Capital
Antigua and Barbuda	St. John's
Bahamas	Nassau
Barbados	Bridgetown
Belize	Belmopan
Canada	Ottawa
Costa Rica	San Jose
Cuba	Havana
Dominica	Roseau
Dominican Republic	Santo Domingo
El Salvador	San Salvador
Grenada	St. George's
Guatemala	Guatemala City
Haiti	Port-au-Prince
Honduras	Tegucigalpa
Jamaica	Kingston
Mexico	Mexico City
Nicaragua	Managua
Panama	Panama City
St. Christopher and Nevis	Basseterre
St.Lucia	Castries
St. Vincent and the Grenadines	Kingstown
Trinidad and Tobago	Port-of-Spain
United States	Washington, D.C.

375. Countries and Capitals of Asia

Country	Capital	Country	Capital
Afghanistan	Kabul	Malaysia	Kuala Lumpur
Bahrain	Manama	Maldives	Male
Bangladesh	Dhaka	Mongolia	Ulan Bator
Bhutan	Thimphu	Nepal	Kathmandu
Brunei	Bandar Seri Begawan	Oman	Muscat
Burma	Rangoon	Pakistan	Islamabad
China	Peking	Philippines	Manila
Cyprus	Nicosia	Qatar	Doha
India	New Delhi	Saudi Arabia	Riyadh
Indonesia	Jakarta	Singapore	Singapore
Iran	Teheran	Sri Lanka	Columbo
Iraq	Baghdad	Syria	Damascus
Israel	Jerusalem	Taiwan	Taipei
Japan	Tokyo	Thailand	Bangkok
Kampuchea	Phnom Penh	Turkey	Ankara
Korea, North	Pyongyang	United Arab Emirates	Abu Dhabi
Korea, South	Seoul	Vietnam	Hanoi
Kuwait	Kuwait	Yemen (Aden)	Aden
Laos	Vientiane	Yemen (Sana)	Sana
Lebanon	Beirut		

Fifteen New Commonwealth of Independent States (formerly the U.S.S.R.)

Country	Capital
Armenia	Yerevan
Azerbaijan	Baku
Byelorussia	Minsk
Estonia	Tallinn
Georgia	Tbilisi
Kazakhstan	Alma Ata
Kirghizia	Frunze
Latvia	Riga
Lithuania	Vilnius
Moldavia	Kishinev
Russia	Moscow
Tadzhikstan	Dushanbe
Turkmenistan	Ashkhabad
Ukraine	Kiev
Uzbekistan	Tashkent

376. Countries and Capitals of Africa

Country	Capital	Country	Capital
Algeria	Algiers	Mauritania	Nauakchott
Angola	Luanda	Morocco	Rabat
Benin	Porto-Novo	Mozambique	Maputo
Botswana	Gaborone	Niger	Niamey
Burkina Faso	Ouagadougou	Nigeria	Lagos
Burundi	Bujumbura	Rwanda	Kigali
Cameroon	Yaoundé	Senegal	Dakar
Cape Verde	Praia	Seychelles	Victoria
Central African	Bangui	Sierra Leone	Freetown
Republic		Somolia	Mogadishu
Chad	N'Djamena	South Africa	Cape Town (legislative)
Comoros	Moroni		Pretoria (administrative)
Congo	Brazzaville		Bloemfontein (judicial)
Djibouti	Djibouti	Sudan	Khartoum
Egypt	Cairo	Swaziland	Mbabane
Gabon	Libreville	Tanzania	Dar es Salaam
Gambia	Banjul	Togo	Lomé
Ghana	Accra	Tunisia	Tunis
Guinea	Conakry	Uganda	Kampala
Guinea-Bissau	Bissau	Zaire	Kinshasa
Ivory Coast	Abidjan	Zambia	Lusaka
Kenya	Nairobi	Zimbabwe	Harare
Lesotho	Maseru		
Liberia	Monrovia		
Madagascar	Antananarivo		
Malawi	Lilongwe		
Mali	Bamako		

377. Countries and Capitals of Europe

County	Capital
Albania	Tiranë
Andorra	Andorra
Austria	Vienna
Belgium	Brussels
Bulgaria	Sofia
Czechoslovakia	Prague
Denmark	Copenhagen
Finland	Helsinki
France	Paris
Germany	Bonn
Great Britain	London
Greece	Athens
Hungary	Budapest
Iceland	Reykjavík
Italy	Rome
Liechtenstein	Vaduz
Luxembourg	Luxembourg
Malta	Valletta
Monaco	Monaco
Netherlands	Amsterdam
Norway	Oslo
Poland	Warsaw
Portugal	Lisbon
Romania	Bucharest
Russia	Moscow
San Marino	San Marino
Spain	Madrid
Sweden	Stockholm
Switzerland	Bern
The Vatican	
Yugoslavia	Belgrade

378. World's Largest Cities

Cairo, Egypt	12,680,000
Mexico City, Mexico	12,650,000
Sãn Paulo, Brazil	12,500,000
Shanghai, China	12,000,000
Seoul, Korea	10,000,000
Beijing, China	10,000,000
Tokyo, Japan	8,540,000
Moscow, USSR	8,500,000
Bombay, India	8,300,000
Jakarta, Indonesia	7,650,000
Canton, China	7,100,000
Tianjin, China	7,020,000
New York City, USA	7,000,000
London, England	6,750,000
Teheran, Iran	6,100,000
Dehli, India	6,000,000
Rio de Janeiro, Brazil	5,700,000
Istanbul, Turkey	5,700,000
Karachi, Pakistan	5,300,000
Shenyang, China	5,250,000
Bangkok, Thailand	5,180,000
Leningrad, USSR	5,000,000
Lima, Peru	4,990,000
Nanking, China	4,700,000
Madras, India	4,400,000

379. Organizations Concerned with the Environment

Acid Rain Foundation
1410 Varsity Drive
Raleigh, NC 27606

Alliance to Save Energy
1725 K Street
#914
Washington, D.C. 20006

American Committee for International Conservation
c/o Sierra Club
408 C Street NE
Washington, D.C. 20002

American Conservation Association
30 Rockefeller Plaza
#5402
New York, NY 10112

American Council on Energy-Efficient Economy
1001 Connecticut Avenue, N.W., #535
Washington, D.C. 20036

American Forestry Association
1516 P Street, N.W.
Washington, D.C. 20036

The American Forum for Global Education
45 John Street, #1200
New York, NY 10038

American Geological Institute
4220 King Street
Alexandria, VA 22302

American Rivers Conservation Council
801 Pennsylvania Avenue, S.E. #303
Washington, D.C. 20003

American Solar Energy Society
850 West Morgan Street
Raleigh, NC 27603

American Water Resources Association
5410 Grosvenor Lane, #220
Bethesda, MD 20814

American Wind Energy Association
1730 North Lynn Street, #610
Arlington, VA 22209

Animal Protection Institute of America
2831 Fruitridge Road
Sacramento, CA 95820

Association of State Drinking Water Administrators
911 North Fort Meyer Drive
Arlington, VA 22209

Association of State and Interstate Water Pollution Control Administration
444 N. Capitol Street, N.W.
Washington, D.C. 20001

Audubon Naturalist Society of the Central Atlantic States
8940 Jones Mill Road
Chevy Chase, MD 20815

Better World Society
1140 Connecticut Avenue, N.W., #1006
Washington, D.C. 20036

Biocycle
Box 351
Emmaus, PA 18049

Bolton Institute for a Sustainable Future
Four Linden Square
Wellesley, MA 02181

Bureau of Mines
U.S. Department of the Interior
2401 E Street, N.W.
Washington, D.C. 20241

Center for Clean Air Policy
444 North Capitol Street, #526
Washington, D.C. 20001

Center for International Development and Environment
1709 New York Avenue, #700
Washington, D.C. 20006

Center for Marine Conservation
1725 DeSales Street, N.W., #500
Washington, D.C. 20036

379. Organizations Concerned with the Environment, continued

Center for Science in the Public Interest
1501 16th Street, N.W.
Washington, D.C. 20036

Citizen's Clearinghouse for
Hazardous Wastes
P.O. Box 926
Arlington, VA 22216

Clean Water Action Project
317 Pennsylvania Avenue, S.E.
Washington, D.C. 20005

Coast Alliance
1536 16th Street, N.W.
Washington, D.C. 20036

Common Cause
2030 M Street, N.W.
Washington, D.C. 20036

Concern Inc.
1794 Columbia Road, N.W.
Washington, D.C. 20009

Congressional Clearinghouse
on the Future
555 House Annex No. 2
Washington, D.C. 20515

The Conservation Foundation
1250 24th Street, N.W. #500
Washington, D.C. 20037

Conservation International
1015 18th Street, N.W. #1000
Washington, D.C. 20036

Coolidge Center for Environmental
Leadership
1675 Massachusetts Avenue, #4
Cambridge, MA 02138

Council on Environmental Quality
722 Jackson Place, N.W.
Washington, D.C. 20006

Council for Solid Waste Solutions
1275 K Street, N.W., #400
Washington, D.C. 20005

Defenders of Wildlife
1244 19th Street, N.W.
Washington, D.C. 20036

Earthwatch Expeditions
1228 31st Street, N.W.
Washington, D.C. 20007

Energy Conservation Coalition
1525 New Hampshire Avenue, N.W.
Washington, D.C. 20036

Environmental Coalition for North
America
1325 G Street, N.W., #1003
Washington, D.C. 20005

Environmental Defense Fund
257 Park Avenue South
New York, NY 10010

Environmental and Energy Study
Institute
122 C Street, N.W., #700
Washington, D.C. 20001

Environmental Hazards Management
Institute
10 Newmarket Road
P.O. Box 932
Durham, NH 03824

Environmental Policy Institute
218 D Street, S.E.
Washington, D.C. 20003

Environmental Task Force
1012 14th Street, N.W., 15th Floor
Washington, D.C. 20005

Freshwater Foundation
2500 Shadywood Road, Box 90
Navarre, MN 55392

Friends of the Earth
218 D. Street, S.E.
Washington, D.C. 20003

Global Action Network
P.O. Box 819
Ketchum, ID 83340

379. Organizations Concerned with the Environment, continued

Goldman Environmental Foundation
1090 Sansome St., 3rd Floor
San Francisco, CA 94111

Greenhouse Crisis Foundation
1130 17th Street, NW #630
Washington, D.C. 20036

Greenpeace USA
1436 U Street, N.W.
Washington, D.C. 20009

Institute for Alternative Agriculture
9200 Edmonston Road, #117
Greenbelt, MD 20770

Institute for Alternative Futures
108 North Alfred Street
Alexandria, VA 22314

Institute for the Study of Natural Systems
26 High Street
Rockport, MA 01966

International Environmental Education Foundation
P.O. Box 1092
Estes Park, CO 80517

International Marine Life Alliance USA
94 Station Street, #1645
Hingham, MA 02043

Keep America Beautiful, Inc.
Mill River Plaza
9 West Broad Street
Stamford, CT 06902

National Audubon Society
950 Third Avenue
New York, NY 10022

National Clean Air Coalition
801 Pennsylvania Avenue, S.E.
Washington, D.C. 20003

National Coalition Against the Misuse of Pesticides
530 7th Street, S.E.
Washington, D.C. 20001

National Geographic Society
17th and M Streets, N.W.
Washington, D.C. 20036

National Parks and Conservation Association
1015 31st Street, N.W., 4th Floor
Washington, D.C. 20007

National Recycling Coalition
P.O. Box 80729
Lincoln, NE 68729

National Wildlife Federation
1400 16th Street, N.W.
Washington, D.C. 20036

National Resources Council of America
1015 31st Street, N.W.
Washington, D.C. 20007

Natural Resources Defense Council
40 West 20th Street
New York, NY 10011

National Clean Air Coalition
801 Pennsylvania Avenue, S.E.
Washington, D.C. 20003

National Toxics Campaign
29 Temple Place, 5th Floor
Boston, MA 02111

The Nature Conservancy
1815 North Lynn Street
Arlington, VA 22209

North American Association for Environmental Education
P.O. Box 400
Troy, NY 45373

The Oceanic Society
218 D Street, S.E.
Washington, D.C. 20003

Panos Institute
1405 King Street
Alexander, VA 22314

379. Organizations Concerned with the Environment, continued

Planet Earth Foundation
2701 First Avenue, #400
Seattle, WA 98121

Rachel Carson Council
8940 Jones Mill Road
Chevy Chase, MD 20815

Rainforest Action Network
301 Broadway, A
San Francisco, CA 94133

Rainforest Alliance
295 Madison Avenue, #1804
New York, NY 10017

Renew America
1400 16th Street, #710
Washington, D.C. 20036

Rural American
1346 Connecticut Avenue, N.W.
Washington, D.C. 20036

Safe Energy Communication Council
1717 Massachusetts Avenue, N.W.
Washington, D.C. 20036

Scenic Shoreline Preservation Conference
4623 More Mesa Drive
Santa Barbara, CA 93110

Sierra Club
530 Bush Street
San Francisco, CA 94108

Soil and Water Conservation Society
7515 Northeast Ankeny Road
Ankeny, IA 50021

Student Conservation Association
P.O. Box 5500
Charlestown, NH 03603

Survival International USA
2121 Decatur Place, N.W.
Washington, D.C. 20008

Tree People
12601 Mulholland Drive
Beverly Hills, CA 90210

United Nations Environment Program
1889 F Street, N.W.
Washington, D.C. 20006

*U.S. Departent of Energy
Conservation and Renewable Energy
Division*
1000 Indepedence Avenue, S.W.
Washington, D.C. 20585

U.S. Environmental Protection Agency
401 M Street, S.W.
Washington, D.C. 20460

Water Pollution Control Federation
601 Wythe Street
Alexandria, VA 22314

Wilderness Society
1400 I Street, N.W., 10th Floor
Washington, D.C. 20005

Work on Waste
82 Judson Street
Canton, NY 13617

World Citizens
312 Sutter Street, #506
San Francisco, CA 94108

Appendix   NEW LISTS

380.   The Europeans Brought to the Americas
(World History)

barley
carnation
chicken
Christianity
coffee
cow
crab grass
daffodil
daisy
dandelion

diphtheria
honeybee
horse
lemon
lettuce
malaria
measles
olive
orange
peach

pear
pig
rice
sheep
smallpox
tulip
turnip
wheat

381.   The Old World Obtained from the Americas
(World History)

avocado
bell pepper
cashew
chilli pepper
cacao (chocolate)
corn
kidney beans
lima beans
marigold

navy beans
peanut
pecan
pineapple
poinsettia
potato
pumpkin
quinine
squash

sunflower
sweet potato
syphilis
tobacco
tomato
turkey
vanilla

382.   Mohandas Gandhi's List of Seven Deadly Sins
(Sociology)

Pleasure without conscience
Wealth without work
Knowledge without character
Worship without sacrifice
Politics without principle
Business without morality
Science without humanity

383. Migraine Headache Sufferers
(Psychology)

Alexander Graham Bell
Lewis Carroll
Frederic Chopin
Charles Darwin
George Eliot
Sigmund Freud
Ulysses S. Grant
Thomas Jefferson
Immanuel Kant
Friedrich Nietzsche
Edgar Allan Poe